PAUL BEW was born in Belfast in 1950. He studied History at Cambridge and is now lecturer in the Political Science Department at Queen's University Belfast. His publications include *Land and the National Question* (1978), *Parnell* (1980), and (with P. Gibbon and H. Patterson) *The State in Northern Ireland: Political Forces and Social Classes 1921–72* (1979). He is co-author with Henry Patterson of *Seán Lemass and the Making of Modern Ireland* (1982).

HENRY PATTERSON was born in Coleraine in 1947. Educated at Queen's University Belfast and Nuffield College, Oxford, he is lecturer in Politics at the University of Ulster. His publications include *Class Conflict and Sectarianism* (1980),*The State in Northern Ireland: Political Forces and Social Classes 1921–72* (1979) and *Seán Lemass and the Making of Modern Ireland* (1982).

Paul Bew
and
Henry Patterson

Verso

The British State and the Ulster Crisis
From Wilson to Thatcher

Verso is the imprint of **New Left Books**

British Library
Cataloguing in Publication Data

Bew, Paul
  The British state and Ulster crisis: from
  Wilson to Thatcher.
  1. Northern Ireland—Politics and government—
  1969–
  I. Title II. Patterson, Henry

First published 1985
© Paul Bew and Henry Patterson

Verso

UK: 6 Meard Street, London W1F 0EG
USA: 20 Jay Street, Suite 1010, Brooklyn, NY 11201

www.versobooks.com

Filmset in 10/12pt Palatino by
PRG Graphics Ltd
Redhill, Surrey

ISBN: 978-0-86091-815-8

Contents

Acknowledgements

The original research on which this book is based was part of the SSRC financed project 'Direct Rule in Northern Ireland 1972–1980' which was conducted by us, and by our colleagues at the Ulster Polytechnic, from May 1981 to May 1983. We are particularly grateful for the assistance of Dennis Norman, Research Officer for the project. Paddy Devlin generously made available his fascinating private collection of materials on the SDLP and other crucial developments. We benefitted from the assistance of politicians and civil servants, some of whom do not wish to be formally acknowledged. Others who assisted us were Peter Melchett, Roger Darlington, Don Concannon, Sydney Elliott, Andy Wilson and Brian Conway. Francis and Clara Mulhern, Neil Belton, Peter Gibbon and Alan Robinson have all read and commented usefully on the manuscript. None of the above has any responsibility for the positions and interpretations of the authors. Finally we would like to acknowledge the continuous encouragement and help from Neil Belton whose enthusiasm was a major stimulus to our writing.

Paul Bew and Henry Patterson
Belfast, February 1985

Introduction

A decade ago in his influential textbook, *Ireland Since the Famine*, FSL Lyons commented: 'At the present moment, with the entrails of Ulster bigotry laid bare to the world as never before, it is perhaps easier to understand the reality of this religious tension, though it is still difficult to explain it.'[1] The chapter in which this statement appears was in fact begun in February 1969, on the day of a decisive general election. On that day, the position of the Unionist Prime Minister, Terence O'Neill, who has been regarded by most writers on Ulster as a liberal reformer, was significantly weakened.[2] In his own constituency, O'Neill was opposed by Ian Paisley, the fundamentalist Protestant leader, whose electoral campaign had combined populist attacks on the Unionist Establishment with allegations that the government was selling out to Dublin. Lyons referred to it as ' . . . the most important general election in its (Ulster's) history, the paramount issue being whether or not Ulster men would at last turn their backs on the sectarianism which had poisoned the history of their province for so many generations.'[3]

Since then O'Neill, like other Unionist Prime Ministers, has been caught between British pressure for reform and the intransigence of many of his supporters. The deepening crisis in Northern Ireland after 1969 eventually led Britain to assume direct responsibility for the government of the province in March 1972. The subsequent period has witnessed the disintegration of the Unionist Party and the rise of the Democratic Unionist Party, which serves to express the view of Ian Paisley and his supporters. The DUP now rivals the Official Unionist party, the direct descendant of the party which controlled the local state for fifty years, for the role of dominant political force in the Protestant community.

Catholic politics in Ulster was also changing. With the rise of the Civil Rights movement in the mid sixties, it seemed as if less emphasis would be placed in future on the question of the legitimacy of the state; a new social democratic reformism, aimed at improving the position of the Catholic population, would emerge. In 1970, the Social Democratic and Labour Party (SDLP) was founded. The emergence of the SDLP, fundamentally reformist in attitude but committed in the long term to a united Ireland, was taken by many to be a sign of a clean break with the politics of the ghetto. Since then, however, the SDLP has assumed a manifestly more traditional approach to the primacy of the national question and has shed some of its most articulate modernisers, including Gerry Fitt and Paddy Devlin. Its decision, during the 1981 hunger strikes, not to oppose IRA hunger striker Bobby Sands in the Fermanagh-South Tyrone by-election undoubtedly reflected a revival of nationalist fervour, with traditional religious overtones, amongst Catholics in Ulster.

In their evaluation of these depressing developments, many commentators on Irish politics have unfortunately adopted an unduly historicist perspective. If, therefore, one interprets Irish history in terms of a fundamental continuity, one has the impression that historical identity cards were handed out at some point in the seventeenth century, about the time of the Plantation of Ulster, and that latter day actors have had no choice but to act out the roles assigned to them by history. Paisleyism has been interpreted as the very essence of Protestant recidivism, a return to a bigoted past. Robert Kee, for instance, has described Paisley as a 'historical throwback to the Presbyterian dissenting radicals of the nineteenth century.'[4] This is to disregard a number of important discontinuities in the history of the Protestant population in Ulster. Most obviously, it fails to take into account the fact that the nationalist uprising of the United Irishmen in 1798 had substantial Presbyterian support. Moreover, in the nineteenth century, Presbyterian radicals stood for something which is anathema to Paisleyism — not national independence, but the construction of a democratic and reformist alliance with Catholics.[5]

Paisleyism is not a simple manifestation of primeval tendencies in the Protestant population; as a mass force it is the creation of political factors which have come into existence since 1968. It is too easy and too convenient for policymakers concerned with Northern Ireland to attribute malevolent tendencies in local politics to the strength of communal sectarian traditions. We shall argue here that British policy, especially since the imposition of Direct Rule in 1972, has done much to bring such traditions to the forefront of politics. An explanation of these developments must examine:

> The nature of the Unionist state and the reasons for its disintegration;
>
> British government policy towards Northern Ireland, particularly since the intensification of the crisis in 1969;
>
> The effects of this policy on internal political forces.

We will argue that the unintentional effects of British policy have been to exacerbate sectarian conflict between Catholics and Protestants.

The State and Sectarianism

It must be stressed that the Unionist mobilisation against Home Rule, at the end of the nineteenth century, and during the first two decades of this century, was not predominantly an Orange Order affair.[6] Despite its importance, the Order was never a force that could have provided an integrating ideology for Unionism as a mass movement. There were simply too many Protestants who not only were not members of it, but were in fact quite hostile towards it. The original unity of the Unionist movement was based on much more than the sectarianism of the Orange Order.

The ideological basis for Unionism was provided by the representation of Ireland's uneven development, which was such a stark reality at the beginning of this century. Unionism was built round the contrast between bustling progressive industrial Ulster and 'backward', 'stagnant' peasant southern Ireland.[7] The

political argument was that rule from Dublin would be econom-
ically and socially retrogressive; this was of particular importance in integrating the Protestant working class into the
Unionist movement.[8] The clear divergence between the
economic and social structures of north and south is sufficient to
account for the emergence of two states and the fact that Protestants, especially in the working class, have always been militantly antinationalist. The role of sectarianism was less in *found-
ing* the state than in influencing the *form* that it took. Whilst
sectarianism should certainly be regarded as a factor affecting
the politics of the Protestant community in any given period, its
importance will always be determined by specific circumstances
and it should therefore be accorded no predetermined significance.

The state of Ulster was born in circumstances of intense political instability. By 1920 it was clear that the IRA had broken
British rule throughout the south of Ireland, whilst in the north,
the Unionist political leadership had become acutely apprehen-
sive about the threat of republicanism. It was also becoming
apparent that the British government hoped to strengthen the
more moderate wing of the nationalist movement, which held
office in Dublin, and was therefore prepared to sacrifice the
Unionists.[9] This made necessary the maximum possible degree
of Unionist unity and, given the lack of trust in Britain's long
term intentions towards the new state, it meant an increasing
reliance on a police force and a special constabulary under local
control and responsive to local Protestant pressures. The
adoption of a more stridently anti-Catholic position by Unionist
politicians was part of the same strategy for maximizing Protestant unity.

The continued existence of the IRA (although during most of
the state's history it had been too feeble to be considered a real
threat), and the almost total consensus in the south that partition
should be ended, gave some external and internal basis for the
Unionist 'siege mentality.' But it was the functioning of the
Unionist state itself — the infamous 'Protestant Parliament for a
Protestant People' — which was largely responsible for that
mentality. By openly demonstrating its distrust of Catholics, by
excluding them, with rare exceptions, from all but the most

menial types of government employment, and by maintaining a form of exceptional legislation (the Special Powers Act) and an often openly partisan judicial system, it demonstrated to the Protestant population just how seriously it took the threat of Catholic subversion.

When the Civil Rights movement emerged, O'Neill and later Unionist leaders who, under British pressure, attempted to reform the state, soon came up against the basic problem that it was this very state and its method of operation that had provided the basis for Unionist unity. The fact that the reforms had been instituted by Britain made the process even more explosive, for the original form of the state had been greatly influenced by Unionist distrust of the British government. It was clear, even by 1921, that Northern Ireland would remain in the United Kingdom, more because of the immense difficulties involved in engineering a united Ireland than from any substantial British interest in maintaining partition. In 1966 at the start of the present 'Troubles', British subsidies to Northern Ireland were approximately £245 per capita (at 1975 prices); by 1978, they had risen to £480.[10] British politicians' reminders of the extent to which the province remains dependent on British support, most notoriously in Harold Wilson's use of the term 'spongers' in his television broadcast during the Ulster Workers' Council strike, have served to accentuate the Protestant fear that any British government will be eager to extricate itself from such a costly commitment.

Those Unionist leaders who have co-operated with British initiatives since 1968 have laid themselves open to the charge of dividing the Protestant community precisely when it most needed to be united. The fact that these reforms concerned, among other things, just those instruments (police and the special constabulary) that had been traditionally defined as essential to the very existence of the state only intensified the opposition. The street violence which erupted in August 1969, and in which members of the special constabulary were involved, precipitated the sending of British troops and created the conditions for the final crisis of the Unionist state.

6

NOTES

1. F S L Lyons, *Ireland Since the Famine*, (London 1971) p. 287.
2. For a critique of this view see Paul Bew, Peter Gibbon and Henry Patterson, *The State in Northern Ireland 1921–72*, (Manchester and New York 1979)
3. Lyons, p. 287.
4. Robert Kee, *Ireland* (London 1981) p. 8.
5. Paul Bew and Frank Wright, 'Agrarian Opposition in Ulster 1848–1887' in *Irish Peasants*, ed Sam Clark and James Donnelly, Wisconsin University Press, 1982.
6. See Peter Gibbon, *The Origins of Ulster Unionism*, (Manchester 1975). The Orange Order was founded in the 1790s as an organisation appealing mostly to the lower classes and advocating Protestant supremacy.
7. Ibid.
8. Henry Patterson, *Class Conflict and Sectarianism: The Protestant Working Class and the Belfast Labour Movement*, (Belfast 1980),
9. Bew *et al*, chapter 2.
10. Bob Rowthorn, 'Northern Ireland: an Economy in Crisis', *Cambridge Journal of Economics* 5 (1981), p. 23.

1

The Failure of Modernisation
1964 – 1971

In 1964 there appeared to be a unique synchronization of the rhythms of British and Northern Irish political developments. The return of the first Wilson government, which was committed to the energetic modernisation of the British economy, and to the rooting out of the amateurish 'Edwardian establishment mentality,'[1] came a few months after Terence O'Neill, Ulster's new prime minister, had reshuffled his cabinet to remove opposition to the creation of a Ministry of Development. This new Ministry was to be a central part of his strategy of 'transforming the face of Ulster.'[2] In January 1965 O'Neill invited the prime minister of the Republic, Seán Lemass, to come north and meet him to discuss 'matters of common concern.'[3] Lemass, the leader of the predominant party in the Republic, Fianna Fail, was already closely associated with crucial new departures in economic policy, the central import of which was to break with the autarchy of three decades. During his period of leadership the 'national question' ceased to be the central issue, ideologically speaking, for Fianna Fail.[4]

The meeting between O'Neill and Lemass appeared to many observers to represent the beginning of a new era in Anglo-Irish and Belfast-Dublin relations. There was, it seemed, only one problem, namely, the relationship of the northern state to the Catholic population. However, even in this area O'Neill's version of modernisation ideology seemed to offer an answer: complaints about Unionist oppression and discrimation were, like the sectarian out-pourings of Protestant evangelicals, a historical residue and, as such, would be increasingly marginalised by his new strategy.

What might have been only a superficial similarity of ideological themes was made more significant by the nature of the relationship between the metropolitan ruling class and what was, in constitutional terms, a mere set of devolved institutions. The context has been well summed up by a senior Ulster civil servant: 'History teaches very simplified lessons. The relevant lesson learnt from Irish history by Great Britain derives from a long drawn out defeat. The residual "lesson" learnt much too well, was that Ireland entails trouble of an unintelligible kind and that on the whole the island is politically hostile. The attitude tends to be applied to Northern Ireland as much as to the Republic.'[6]

Of course this process of psychological withdrawal was not unwelcome to the Unionist regime, as it allowed them considerable freedom in the ordering of political relations in Northern Ireland. Even after 1945, when financial relations between the Northern Ireland state and the Treasury were altered to allow both the extension of the welfare state to the province and to increase the level of government capital expenditure,[7] the Labour government, through the Home Secretary, made it clear that it was going to ignore attempts by the 'Friends of Ireland' group of Labour back-benchers to raise issues such as electoral law malpractices, discrimination and the Special Powers Act in Ulster.[8]

Here a distaste for involvement in Ulster was accompanied by a general reluctance, on the part of the English ruling-class, to appear to take sides against the northern government, which was seen as having 'done its bit' during the war, in contrast to the government in the south, which had remained neutral.[9] When the Irish coalition government in 1948 decided to leave the Commonwealth and declare a Republic, the Attlee administration, eager to demonstrate that it was as staunch a defender of Britain's imperial role as any Tory administration, and to allay the anxiety of people of Northern Ireland, took a firm line in favour of partition.

The British state's attitude to Ulster was in part determined by strategic considerations, as was made quite plain at the time. On 16 October 1947, Lord Rugby, the British representative in

Dublin, told De Valera, the prime-minister and leader of Fianna Fail:

> If he desired to work towards a solution (ie of partition) here and now his best plan would be to make it clear that Eire was not blind to the strategic lessons of history which had been re-emphasised in the last war and that she was prepared to play her part. Mr De Valera as usual attempted to rebut the argument that any portion of Ireland could involve the United Kingdom in any danger. I said that we were not taking any risks about that. The last war had taught us a lesson.[10]

De Valera then posed the obvious question:

> He then asked whether, if the North were prepared to come willingly into Eire, we should allow them to do so. I said that most certainly we should, though presumably the strategic factor of our narrow seas should have to be covered by some specific arrangement unless some wider understanding made this unnecessary. We should not forget our jugular vein.[11]

By 1949 the British position had hardened somewhat. The Labour government received this civil service recommendation: 'It has become a matter of strategic importance to this country that the North (of Ireland) should continue to form part of his Majesty's Dominions. So far as it can be foreseen, it will never be to Great Britain's advantage that Northern Ireland should form a territory outside his Majesty's jurisdiction. Indeed, it would seem unlikely that Great Britain would ever be able to agree to this even if the people of Northern Ireland desired it.'[12]

The result of this was the 1949 Ireland Act, which for the first time gave statutory assurance that Northern Ireland would not cease to be part of the United Kingdom without the consent of the Northern parliament. Although 66 Labour MP s defied the whips and opposed the legislation,[13] the variegated nature of their positions demonstrated the weakness of the anti-Unionist position in the party. The main division was between those who took a traditional nationalist line and collaborated with the Anti-Partition League, an organization set up in Ulster in 1945 to campaign for a united Ireland; and a larger group who were simply concerned that 'British' standards of democracy and justice did not exist in Northern Ireland. As the southern state entered a period of acute economic crisis, which appeared to undermine its political independence,[14] it became less and less feasible to imagine 'solving' the problems of the North by incorporating it into the South. In fact, as a recent study of the Labour 'Friends of Ireland' group has noted of Geoffrey Bing's *John Bull's Other Ireland*, its most significant publication: 'To Bing the British connection, far from being unalterably a pillar of sectarian rule in Northern Ireland, was the most likely source of progressive political change, which was synonymous with economic development.'[15]

It was also necessary to decide which political forces in the north should be supported. Whilst the war years had seen an increase in support for the small Northern Ireland Labour Party, which had won two Stormont seats and 18% of the vote in 1945,[16] it had, by contrast with the nationalist Anti-Partition League, no representation at Westminster. The alliance with the nationalists was therefore, in practice, the predominant one. However, once the Ireland Act was passed the APL turned against the Labour party and began to sponsor anti-Labour candidates in British constituencies with a significant Irish vote.[17] By this time the NILP had split on the question of support for the Union with Britain and was not to recover its post-war position until the end of the fifties. As the main southern parties which had sponsored the anti-partition campaign became increasingly preoccupied with economic policy, and as northern nationalists abandoned hope of persuading the Labour government to re-open the question of constitutional relations between the three states, the pressures which had raised Ulster as an issue at Westminster receded and with them the interest of all but a few backbenchers in either Irish state.

When, therefore, the Wilson government came to power, it was unencumbered by anything that could properly be described as a Northern Ireland policy. The ignominious collapse of the IRA's military campaign to end partition (1956-62), the Fianna Fail government's active role in repressing the IRA itself, and Lemass's subsequent eagerness to improve and liberalise trading relations with Britain, seemed to indicate that the Irish Question as traditionally posed was no longer pertinent.

Lemass's attitude to partition — that northerners could only be attracted by a higher economic standard of life in the Republic[18] — clearly signified a gradualist approach. The presence of a substantial Irish population in Harold Wilson's own constituency had caused him to give expression to arguments in favour of unity; some Unionists were naturally a little alarmed. However, his policies on the two Irish states were in fact quite distinct. Symbolic gestures, such as the return of the remains of Sir Roger Casement in February 1965,[19] were linked to the negotiations which culminated in the Anglo-Irish Free Trade Agreement (January 1966), and were seen as part of a process of improving Anglo-Irish relations, but none of these developments were felt to have any implications for the north.

Shortly before the 1964 general election Harold Wilson had written to one of the middle class Catholics who were shortly to found the Campaign for Social Justice in Northern Ireland; he stated that, if elected, he would implement large scale changes in Northern Ireland.[20] In office he showed a surprising readiness to accept O'Neill's claims to be engaged in a courageous attempt to reconstruct the north's political system. He writes of a meeting with O'Neill in May 1965

> . . . . I was anxious that the Ulster Unionist government under Captain O'Neill should be encouraged to press on with their programme of ending discrimination in housing allocations and jobs and generally improving the lot of the minority of Northern Ireland. Since coming into office he had by Northern Ireland standards, carried through a remarkable programme of easement.[21]

This statement has a double significance. First, it betrays a fundamental misunderstanding of the policies of the O'Neill government during this period. As we have demonstrated at greater length elsewhere,[22] O'Neill hoped, through his rhetoric of 'planning' and 'modernisation', to re-establish the Unionist party's hegemony over the Protestant working class. He had done absolutely nothing to counter discrimination against Catholics in Northern Ireland. Wilson's failure to understand O'Neill is in part attributable to the pro-Unionist positions of the Home Office officials, since they provided one of the main channels of communication between the two states.[23] However, perhaps more significantly for the subsequent development of British policy under both Labour and Conservative administrations, there was a sense in which the *effects* of O'Neillite policies were potentially to transform the relationship of the central state apparatus to some of the most politically crucial forms of sectarian discrimination. As the most systematic and judicious of the analyses of this issue puts it,

> A group of local authorities in the west of the province provide a startingly high proportion of the total number of complaints. All the accusations of gerrymandering, practically all the complaints about housing and regional policy, and a disproportionate amount of the charges about private and public employment come from this area.[24]

During his period of government, O'Neill attempted to centralise initiative with a relatively small number of ministers and civil servants at Stormont, an alteration which might have eliminated these less savoury aspects of the local state. For although the Northern Ireland Civil Service was, as we shall see, markedly affected by sectarianism, sections of it had provided the most substantial bases for non-sectarian administration under the Unionist regime.[25] Perhaps even more important it was amongst the bureaucracy that the need to take account of cross-channel expectations (of 'British' standards) was most developed, for it was at this level that there was the most contact between the two states. The effect of O'Neill's policies was therefore to create tensions between his government and some of the most backward elements of the Unionist party, and this allowed him to represent himself as a progressive force whilst in fact no actual strategy of reforming sectarian relations existed. This, together with the existence in the bureaucracy of a group at the highest level who were recognised as at least passably 'British' in terms of standards of competence and non-partisanship, was to be the rather insubstantial basis on which Wilson's hopes of change were to rest.

Wilson's relationship to O'Neill also tells us much about the British party's relationship to labourist politics in the North. Indeed, labourist politics, in the form of the NILP, had been experiencing a degree of electoral success.[26] The NILP was bitterly dismissive of O'Neill's modernising rhetoric, for it had learnt how hollow it was at the time of the 1965 election for Stormont; when O'Neill had conducted a personal campaign against its MPs, employing the traditional line of argument that they were supporters of the English Prime Minister, Harold Wilson, who he claimed was a committed nationalist.[27] The British Labour Party, which treated its own arrival as the 'natural party of government' as part of some ineluctable process going with the grain of its 'national' history, could only think of a party as weak as the NILP in terms of an unalterable otherness, rooted in a reality, that of 'Irish' history, which generally served as a justi- fication for refusing to think any further. As a result, sectarian- ism and the multifarious nature of communal division were treated as effectively trans-historical realities, and the crucial question of the role of the state in their reproduction was never posed. This would have more than intellectual consequences, since the existing state apparatus was deeply implicated in the creation of sectarian division, and a strategy of reform which relied on the facile notion of a division between liberalising reformists and 'right wing extremists,'[28] grossly exaggerated the degree to which O'Neill had either the will or the capacity to alter substantially the main dynamics of the regime.

In November 1966 Roy Jenkins, who was Home Secretary, told a delegation from the backbench pressure group, the Campaign for Democracy in Ulster, that the government was pressing the Stormont regime to bring in reforms.[29] Such pressure did not extend to visiting the north to observe progress — between Labour's return to office in 1964 and August 1969 only one minister, Home Secretary Sir Frank Soskice, visited the province and that only for an afternoon.[30] The achievements of O'Neill's government prior to 1968 could in fact be described as symbolic gestures — the détente with the Republic which his meeting with Lemass represented, or the occasional visit to a convent school — or as modernisations of a technocratic sort — such as the reforms of local government which were begun in early 1966. As one of the civil servants involved in drafting them has sub- sequently pointed out, they were aimed at the 'antiquated, . . . wasteful and confusing' characteristics of the existing system, and sought to replace it with a 'simplified, single tier, strong local government system with a full range of powers including housing.'[31] Even if the reforms which the civil rights movement was demanding in the local government electoral system had also been contemplated at this time (and they were not) the new system would not have removed one of the most important features of the Unionist local state, namely, allocation of public authority housing.

Wilson thus fundamentally misunderstood the nature of the opposition to O'Neill, concluding from its vociferousness that O'Neill was actually capable of dealing with Catholic grievances. In fact the emergence of serious divisions among the Unionists by 1966, demonstrated that O'Neill was not about to bring about the first tentative improvements in relations between the Protestant and Catholic communities. It was rather that sectarianism was being displaced, so that it appeared to be a matter of 'culture' and 'tradition', whilst politics was redefined in terms of technical and administrative capacity. This would have necessitated not merely a re-organisation of the relations between the state apparatuses at central and local level, but also a recomposition of the dominant ideology, such that technocratic themes — economic growth, state-sponsored modernisation etc displaced sectarian ones, without of course eliminating them. Such a reconstruction of the Unionist system was not doomed to failure. The crucial pre-requisite for its success was the capacity of the traditional political parties — Unionist and Nationalist — to maintain their control of the masses.

The Nationalist party was the weak link here. It had responded very favourably to O'Neill's gestures and in 1965 had reciprocated by accepting the role of official opposition at Stormont. This was to have much less effect on Catholic politics than O'Neill might have hoped, as the party's support base was predominantly rural, and urban Catholics had throughout the post-war period supported a variety of republican, republican-labour and even NILP politicians.[32] Thus while there is some evidence that a substantial proportion of the Catholic middle class was prepared to support O'Neill's policies, the return of the Labour government, its modernising ideology and the existence from the middle of 1965 of a backbench pressure group — the

Campaign for Democracy in Ulster — with a substantial membership within a year, created an atmosphere in which the space for a much more militant, if 'responsible' reform movement was created.

It was only three years later, however, after Wilson had consistently responded to CDU pressure for action with statements of support for O'Neill's supposed attempts to reform, that this reform movement gathered any real momentum.[33] Wilson's failure to examine seriously O'Neill's policies may, ironically enough, be held in large part responsible for the eventual collapse of O'Neill's government. These policies could only have succeeded if there had been an early implementation of reforms in the area of local government and housing. Wilson interpreted O'Neill's unpopularity with sections of the Unionist party as a sign that he was gradually reconciling Catholics to the Stormont regime. The fact is, however, that O'Neill's rather nebulous plans for local government reform — despite the intense opposition they aroused from local Unionist organisations — did not appear likely to demolish even the most blatantly sectarian authorities, and thus won more support for the tactics of the Northern Ireland Civil Rights Association (founded January 1967), which increasingly functioned to demonstrate the limitations and contradictions of his policies.

O'Neill hoped to establish a more centralised and bureaucratised Unionist regime, in which the traditional populism of Unionist politics would have had a secondary role, and in which a decisive majority of Catholics would have been reconciled to the regime, through appealing by and large to their self-interest.

O'Neill's policies need not necessarily have failed.[34] It was his very success in impressing Wilson with his modernising zeal that, by removing pressure for an early intervention in the crucial area of local government reforms, contributed to the civil rights mobilisation that sealed its fate. O'Neill's position within Unionism was tenable only as long as reforms were restricted in their scope and left the ideologically crucial security apparatuses untouched.

Once the civil rights movement was forced to adopt more public manifestations of opposition, from the middle of 1968, O'Neill's position became increasingly precarious. For a while his earlier plan for the reform of local government had been opposed vehemently by representatives of the local Unionist political machines but did not inflame the Protestant masses. However, the decision to hold protest marches and not to recognise the legitimacy of sectarian territorial divisions assured the irruption of just those aspects of popular Protestant sectarianism which his whole project was designed to consign to a mute and a-political existence. O'Neill's policies could only have succeeded if the Protestant masses had remained passive. The confrontation between civil rights marchers and the police in Derry in October 1968, the RUC's brutal dispersal of the march, and the moving of the question of reform of the state's security apparatuses to the centre of the civil rights movements' demands, changed popular Protestant conceptions of the issues at stake.[35]

O'Neill had relied on an ideology of modernisation to justify his policies to the Unionist party's traditional support base. They were represented as building on the past 'achievements' of the Unionist regime, whilst transforming its public image to make it more attractive to external investors and public opinion in Britain. By the end of 1968 it was clear that his programme had not been successful in ameliorating Catholic grievances, whilst at the same time the behaviour of the police was leading to intensifying demands at Westminister for a more thoroughgoing set of reforms. The initiative had clearly been lost. Whilst, in his first year of office, O'Neill had won back some of the Unionist party's prestige, by identifying his government as an active agent of change, it was now apparent that he was simply the passive object of pressures from NICRA and the Wilson administration. It was not the nature of the reforms which O'Neill had proposed which undermined his government for, by the time he had resigned (April 1969) the crucial mobilising demand of the civil rights movement — 'one man one vote' in local government elections — had been conceded. It was rather, as his most articulate critic in the party, Brian Faulkner, recognised, O'Neill's designation of the Unionist Party as, in effect, a reactionary obstacle that had led to a situation in which his opponents could link opposition to reforms to claims that the real effect of his policies would be to destroy the Party itself. To characterise the division in the party as a left/right or a liberal/reactionary one, as was done at the time by both the opposition and the Wilson administration, was to fail to grasp the issues that were at stake. O'Neill himself of course had done much to foster these conceptions of divisions within Unionism. In fact the real division was over the political context in which the reforms would be introduced.

The Unionist regime was presented by O'Neill, in public statements at any rate, as one that would win support through its capacity to respond to 'responsible opinion' in London and thereby to smoothly mediate the benefits of United Kingdom citizenship to Northern Ireland. By the beginning of 1969, however, this had come to seem a somewhat utopian prospect, as O'Neill's opponents realised. For, if the earlier opposition to his modernisation policies could be dismissed as mere localistic particularism, the increasing number of confrontations between civil rights marchers, Protestant counter-demonstrators and the RUC and 'Specials' demonstrated that the opposition to modernism went right to the heart of the central state apparatuses. However, in the aftermath of the Burntollett march, which had served to intensify criticism of the RUC,[36] O'Neill made it clear that there would be strict limits to the 'changing' face of Ulster, and that reforms would leave the repressive apparatuses untouched. This made his whole project incoherent, as it became increasingly obvious that responsiveness to London and defence of the existing security apparatus were incompatible.

O'Neill and his opponents did not therefore differ over what was fast becoming the central issue, namely, reform of the repressive apparatuses. The logic of modernisation did not preclude a reform of the police and 'Specials' and if O'Neill seemed reluctant to tackle this problem, it was because he was still, even when at the end of his tether, subject to a different logic. He was, in short, at the mercy of the populist responsiveness which had always characterised the relationship of the Unionist state apparatuses to the Protestant masses. Nowhere was this more evident than in the case of the repressive apparatuses. It was the contradiction between these two logics which sealed the fate of O'Neill's policies. That O'Neill had argued against some of the most virulent manifestations of Protestant sectarianism is obvious. However, to characterise antagonism to

O'Neill's policies as pure reaction, as Westminster politicians so often did, was altogether too facile and reductive a response, for some of the opposition to his government derived from the contradictory nature of his whole project. It was becoming increasingly clear that to argue that the hallmark of a 'good Unionist' was responsiveness to the interests of the United Kingdom as a whole, and at the same time bovinely to defend those apparatuses which were doing most to incur adverse interest from the British ruling class, was a recipe for incoherence and ineffectuality.

O'Neill resigned within a week of the Unionist parliamentary party voting, by a narrow majority, to allow one-man-one-vote in local government elections. His resignation was quickly followed by the election, as his successor, of his nondescript cousin James Chichester Clark, who had resigned from the cabinet on this very same issue. These events seem to have been part of an attempt to reintegrate some of O'Neill's main opponents into the government and thus to consolidate an 'O'Neillism without O'Neill.'[37] This was clearly the view of the Wilson administration which, despite the obvious doubts as to whether the announced reforms would pacify the civil rights movement, was loath even to contemplate the implications of a popular mobilisation persisting or intensifying. But already the effect of the marches, epitomised above all by the People's Democracy 'Long March' from Belfast to Derry in January, had been to unleash a very traditional dialectic of sectarian confrontation, in which sections of the police and 'Specials' were directly embroiled. There were also signs that the opposition leaders were increasingly unsure of how to react in the intensifying conflict. On the left, the PD decided to give up marching in the North for, as Eamonn McCann, the leading Derry socialist, ingenuously put it, ' . . . the civil rights campaign must acknowledge that it had failed in its primary task of building bridges to the Protestant working class. We have alienated them (Catholics) from their Protestant neighbours more than ever before.' At the same meeting the chief ideologist of PD, Michael Farrell, added: 'The marches already held have been mainly composed of Catholic people. He did not believe they would get civil rights by marching in the streets and attacking the government. They had a choice between "Green Power" and working class unity.'[38]

It was an indication of the degree to which these leftist elements had lost any initiative as the conflict intensified that, less than three weeks later, in an interview with *New Left Review*, Farrell was prepared to consider 'Green Power', now referred to as 'Catholic-based power, of a socialist form', as a serious stategic option.[39] McCann, who was clearly less willing to re-baptise an upsurge of communalism, even that of an oppressed group, as aform of dual power, was disconcertingly frank about the religious tone of at least some of the civil rights confrontations:

> It is perfectly obvious that people do still see themselves as Catholics and Protestants, and the cry 'get the Protestants' is still very much on the lips of the Catholic working class. Everyone applauds loudly when one says in a speech that we are not sectarian, we are fighting for the rights of all Irish workers, but really that's because they see this as the new way of getting at the Protestants.[40]

The leadership of NICRA was also clearly finding it difficult to respond coherently to the growing crisis, and tended to react to each event as it occurred. Thus, on the one hand, it made hysterical visits to Dublin to ask of Lynch, the Fianna Fail prime minister, that his government demand United Nations intervention and a joint British-Irish military presence in Derry and other trouble spots,[41] on the other, it called off its street campaign after O'Neill had conceded one man one vote.[42] However O'Neill's subsequent resignation and the slender margin of Chichester Clark's victory over Brian Faulkner led to a recrudescence of 'crisis statements.' Two of the most prominent civil rights activists who had been elected to Stormont in February, Bernadette Devlin and Ivan Cooper, demanded direct rule.[43] The Executive of NICRA threatened to resume its marches within six weeks if a timetable for the introduction of the promised reforms were not produced and if a commitment were not made to drop the Special Powers Act and the Public Order Act.[44] NICRA's statement expressed doubts about the administration's ability to act, because of the strength of the 'right' within it. The problem with this type of analysis was that in an important sense it underestimated the extent of the problem. For on the crucial issue of reforms in security policy there was no left or right in the administration. Continuing O'Neill's approach, Chichester Clark could persuade cabinet and party that it was necessary to give a concrete commitment on local government reforms, whilst maintaining an unreconstructed traditionalism as far as security policy was concerned.

However, the relationship between the Wilson administration and the Unionist regime was already changing. By 1969 the modernisation project was in ruins in the rest of the United Kingdom and its collapse in Ulster was therefore all the less likely to be replaced by any coherent alternative strategy. The creation of a cabinet committee on Ulster was not the sign of a realisation of the need for a reappraisal of policy but rather of the need for contingency planning for the increasingly likely deployment of increased numbers of British troops. Support for O'Neill's government had been a substitute for the acquisition of knowledge and the elaboration of a Northern Ireland policy. Although it appears that Wilson was in favour of a more aggressive policy towards the Unionist regime, this does not appear to have been more than a rhetorical commitment, given that he, like all the other members of the committee, was unwilling to contemplate the possible need to displace the Unionist regime itself.[45] The failure of O'Neillism thus served to reinforce that long-standing disposition on the part of the governing class to treat Northern Ireland as an irritating and irresolvable remnant of the 'Irish Question.' Thus, although Wilson was prepared publicly to endorse the new administration's commitment to reform — to the extent of defending its need for continuation of the Special Powers Act[46] Chichester Clark's requests for extra financial assistance for job creation and house building were frostily received. Clearly the Labour administration had convinced itself that its responsibilities to the north were almost exhausted.[47]

In this context it is more appropriate to see the next reform package, produced in the aftermath of the intense violence in Derry and Belfast, which saw the effective collapse of the regime's security apparatus and the introduction of British troops, not as the beginning of some new stage in British involvement, but as a last desperate attempt to limit it. Although at various times over the previous year Wilson had warned that the introduction of troops could not help but have 'constitutional consequences',[48] nothing could have been further from the minds of the Northern Ireland Committee. The result would be, as Wilson notes pathetically, more beneficial in Britain than in the North — leading to a temporary increase in morale for his government: 'the Labour government was seen to be acting with manifest firmness and authority in a demonstrably difficult situation.'[49]

Over the next six months, politicians and civil servants repeatedly asserted that there had been a radical change in the relationship between the two governments. The dispatch of two senior British civil servants — 'to represent the increased concern which the United Kingdom had necessarily acquired in Northern Ireland affairs through the commitment of the armed forces in the present conditions'[50] — was meant to indicate a new level of British involvement. Other initiatives in this period included the creation of joint working parties of British and Stormont officials to consider how discrimination in the fields of public employment and housing could be dealt with, an 'economic mission' to Ulster to expand employment and the creating of a new Northern Ireland department in the Home Office.[51] Together with the appointment of the Hunt Committee to advise on the reform of policing, and the resultant moves to civilianise and disarm the RUC and disband the Specials, these moves encouraged the hopes of those who credited the British state with a capacity for genuine reconstruction. After a section of the civil rights movement had demanded direct rule, a leader writer in the constitutional nationalist *Irish Times* was so captivated by the apparent radicalism of Wilson's intentions as to contemplate benignly a more complete integration of Northern Ireland into the United Kingdom:

> a decade of direct rule by Westminster might change the North so much that, ideologically the Nationalist portion of the population might drop out of the tradition of Irish nationalism . . . If Westminster were to use the North as an example of a new federal system of government, money, ideas and energy would be poured

in to such an extent, the standard of living for everyone could rise so high that the rest of Ireland would be left behind.[52]

However it was soon to be evident that James Callaghan's triumphant visits to the barricaded streets of the Bogside and Falls were little more than a personal publicity coup.[53] He returned to the North in October to register the supposed rapidity of change. The *Irish Times* political correspondent grandiloquently referred to the effect of the measures as the 'fall of feudalism' in the north.[54] The 'new deal', as it was presented, promised a new central housing authority to build and allocate public housing; there was also to be extra finance to fund an emergency building programme. Other items were a £2 million programme of job creation schemes, an increase of 5% in the already high level of investment grants available for industries setting up in the north and a series of measures to deal with discrimination in public employment. Callaghan also announced that the government would accept the recommendations of the Hunt Committee, reform of the RUC and the phasing out of the Specials.[55] Callaghan made it clear that as far as the government was concerned this package should bring pacification: 'his reform package was surely adequate for all fair minded people in the North. The only people who will find fault with it are a small bunch of violent trouble makers.'[56] The reaction to one part of the package — the phasing out of the Specials — was two nights of bitter Protestant rioting on the Shankill Road.

Once these riots had subsided the north entered a period of relative calm. By the beginning of 1970 there was a facile optimism in the cabinet and at Whitehall. It was clearly reflected in an *Irish Times* investigation of the new relations between Stormont and Westminster: 'The British view is that the Northern Ireland problem has "been licked" and that apart from odd scuffles, peace in the streets has been won and that reform will transform the north.'[57] By February 1970 three of the eight additional Army units in the province had returned to Britain.[58]

This optimism would very soon disintegrate. It was based on a fundamental misconception of the true nature of the post-August reforms. Wilson and Callaghan considered that they had been forced by circumstances — the Unionist regime's loss of control of public order — to intervene and to hasten and strengthen the reform programme. This was all that they had ever intended. Direct rule had never even been contemplated: having impelled the Chichester Clark administration to move faster, they believed that a return to something like the traditional relationship would be possible. However, by forcing through the reform of the police and Specials, they had severely weakened the Unionist regime, for they had destroyed the crucial relationship between it and the Protestant masses. At the same time this political disabling of the regime produced an intensely febrile atmosphere in the 'shatter zones' where confrontations between Catholics and Protestants were traditional. The result was the crucial Ballymurphy riots in April 1970.

These riots are usually presented as a watershed, in the sense that they saw the first major conflict between the Catholic working class and the British army.[59] In fact, even more significant for the development of British policy was the occurrence of anti-Protestant expulsions in the near-by New Barnsley estate.[60] These developments brought forth a chorus of condemnation from civil rights leaders, who were clearly aware of the potential damage they could do in undermining support in Britain.[61] It was certainly clear that for those, like Callaghan, who had only the most superficial notions of the forces at play, these events could produce only expressions of pained exasperation. In a Commons debate on the riots, during which the General commanding the British Army had threatened that petrol bombers would be shot, Callaghan made it clear that the Catholic masses had virtually exhausted the sympathies of the government. He supported the General's threat: 'Some hon. Gentlemen may not like the choice of language, but the way to avoid it is very simple. Do not go out with a petrol bomb.' He went on to complain about the 'concentration on the imagined and real grievances at times to the complete exclusion of the measures of progress which are being made in this country.'[62] The origins of current problems, apart from the supposedly 'Irish' inability to be satisfied, were also fatuously ascribed to the '250 or 500 men in Northern Ireland today who are intent on dragging the country down so that it lives under the shadow of the gun.'[63] Coupled with the victory of Paisley and a supporter in two Stormont by-elections, where they defeated Unionist candidates,[64] the riots appear to have convinced Callaghan that activism in British policy was now redundant. As he explained to a Labour Party audience in England, 'Some problems you can't solve, you have to live with. This is one I think we have got to live with.'[65]

'Living with' the problem increasingly meant doing as little as possible to undermine the authority of the Unionist regime, which was at least more amenable to British desires than the masses on both sides. The failure of the post-August reforms was taken to demonstrate the paramount importance of attempting to resist more direct involvement by maintaining some sort of Unionist regime in power. Thus, although during the general election campaign Wilson was to accuse the Tories of being dangerously pro-Unionist in their sympathies,[66] the disastrous decision of the new government not to ban Orange marches at the end of June[67] had been prefigured by the increasingly passive attitude of the Labour government.

It has since been claimed that Wilson and Callaghan had decided to introduce direct rule if they won the general election.[68] This seems unlikely, for Wilson later denied publicly that direct rule had any contribution to make. While the Northern Ireland department in the Home Office would certainly have drawn up contingency plans for direct rule if the Unionist regime had completely disintegrated, there is little evidence of a positive strategic option embracing direct rule. This was because there was so little general agreement as to the purpose of such an intervention. Whereas, for Wilson the interregnum was to be used to create a basis for a new constitutional initiative, Callaghan appears to have reacted quite differently to the worsening situation. In July he was to write to the general secretary of the Labour Party: 'The path to peace in Northern Ireland and to good relations with the government of the Republic lies in bringing together in one party the Protestant and Catholic working class.'[69] The British party should therefore, in his view, have provided the NILP with financial, organisational and moral support. In fact, earlier that year, a special delegate conference of the NILP had voted to support plans for a merger with the BLP and there had been subsequent discussions between officials of both parties.[70] However, the idea that a 'solution' could be achieved by reconstructing the party system on 'British' lines, although it had the support of some Tories, including Quintin Hogg, seemed exotic to most members of the English ruling class, who were still convinced of the unalterable 'otherness' of the Irish, including those in the north. More concretely the 'Troubles' saw a continuous decline in the electoral support for the NILP and when one of its two Stormont MPs became a founder member of the Social Democratic and Labour Party in the autumn of 1970, it was to this party that support from the BLP inevitably gravitated.

When the failure of 'reformism' in Northern Ireland is analysed, writers usually refer to the experience of the Wilson-Callaghan years. What is striking about these discussions is that even those who are critical of the reformism of that period still take its pretensions seriously. Thus we are told that 'British politicians saw nothing wrong with Northern Ireland that could not be cured by a good strong dose of the same social-democratic reformism that had emerged in post-war Britain' and later we are informed of the government's 'enthusiastic commitment to the initial flurry of reform in Northern Ireland.'[71] In fact it is clear that Callaghan only began to think of 'social democratic' solutions after the disintegration of, first, O'Neill's government and then of the post-August reforms. Moreover, neither the O'Neill nor the post-August reforms were meant to produce a 'British' type of consensus. Initially O'Neill's claims to be at least relegating traditional divisions to a secondary place were gratefully and uncritically received. There was never any suggestion that the Unionist/Nationalist division would disappear; there was simply the hope that it would assume a more civilised form of expression. The reforms introduced after the August 1969 conflagration were not, in essence, conceived differently. In so far as they were more radical, this was seen as an inevitable response to a deteriorating situation. Again it was calculated that, as a Unionist regime was still in power, a re-affirmation of support for the existing constitutional framework would probably pacify all but the Protestant extremists. Conversely, the stern and watchful attitude towards the new reforms adopted by Stormont was considered to be guarantee enough for the Catholic masses that things had changed significantly, and in their favour.

Those who formulated this strategy had completely under-estimated the effect of this new British presence inside the Unionist regime. On the Protestant side, it was not conceived, as its Home Office apologists put it, as an index of a strengthening of the Union through breaking down years of mutual insulation and ignorance.[72] The Unionist regime had since its inception emphasised the possible duplicity of British governments and the consequent need for a cohesive and loyal set of state appara-tuses. According to this ideology power was divided in a zero-sum manner. The very presence, in the heart of the Unionist regime, of a 'United Kingdom representative', one of whose main tasks was to keep in close touch with opposition leaders,[73] was taken as an indication that the state itself had ceased to function properly. This reinforced popular Protestant apprehen-sions about the so-called 'No Go' areas: those large swathes of Catholic working-class Belfast and Derry which had erected bar-ricades in August 1969 and which, even after the barricades came down, were run by local 'Citizens' Defence Committees', and from which the RUC was effectively excluded. There was no comfort in the fact that the army could and did enter these areas; the point was that they were not under direct Unionist control. By the end of 1969 the Unionist regime had been fundamentally disarticulated. However, neither Wilson nor Callaghan had any conception of the prior dynamics of the regime, since they enter-tained the misguided notion that its mass basis was the *expres-sion* of historical retardation and not the *creation* of political strategy materialised in a state of a particular type. They there-fore had no conception of just how much damage their reforms did to the regime. It was no longer possible to heal the divisions within the Unionist party and its preservation in power could only lead to a geometrical deterioration in the situation.[74]

The Emergence of the Provisionals

The opposition's response is highly significant here, for it is clear that the strategic implications of the reform programme were increasingly problematical for it. For the left in the civil rights movement the question was put in stark and semi-apocalyptic terms. Michael Farrell argued at a PD meeting in Dublin that the Unionist regime would be unable to implement the reform programme. 'They had had a taste of Orange fascism . . . . The Protestant working class held a privileged position . . . . and they saw with the end of discrimination the end of that privileged position. It was that Protestant backlash which was recruiting for Orange Fascism.'[75] As the British state was *a priori* ruled out as a possible agency of progressive change — 'The root cause went back to British imperialism which created the border' — the 'solution' was simply to invoke a 'socialist workers republic': 'If the people of the country controlled its resources they could provide enough houses and jobs for everyone.' The weakness of ultra-leftist arguments of this kind consisted in their inability to specify in any way how a heightening of the current mobilisations would create the conditions for a subsequent struggle for socialist objectives. Whilst the left could not envisage a British government impelling the introduction of the reforms, the more prominent centrist leaders of the opposition, such as John Hume and Gerry Fitt, remained surprisingly willing to see in the British state a force capable of forcing adaptation on a recalcitrant regime. Thus, in a debate after the Ballymurphy riots, Fitt urged the government to impel the immediate introduction of the post-August reforms. The reform programme itself was not criticised; the major problem, as Fitt saw it, was a possible defeat for Wilson in the general election, which would mean a Tory administration friendly to the Unionists and unwilling to pressure them on reforms.[76] Despite what recent 'revisionist' writing on the nationalist element in the civil rights movement has claimed about its essentially anti-partitionist motivation,[77] it appears that the predominant tendency in the leadership was to see their future as the 'responsible' oppostion to a reformed Unionist regime.[78] In its own way as committed as Wilson, O'Neill and his successor, to notions of a centrally impelled and continuous process of modernisation, the leadership of the opposition was quite unprepared for serious discontinuity involving a crisis of the state itself.

Here we can certainly detect the lingering influence of nationalist ideology. For, as Fitt had made clear in his Commons speech 'the British government have divided the Irish people',[79] the creation and preservation of the Northern state was attributed to British policy, with the mass of the Protestant population a mere catspaw. If the main historical dynamic of Unionist separatism had been externally induced, then it was quite conceivable that reform could be equally well guaranteed from external pressure. Similarly it was believed that opposition to reform came from the 'right wing' of the party. This seriously underestimated the nature of the conflict by failing to perceive that what was at issue was not simply reforms but the whole dynamic of Unionism as a popular force.

As a result the main 'constitutional' opponents of the regime became increasingly obviously dependent on a reluctant pressure from Westminster on the Unionists. But as had become clear in the last months of the Wilson administration, the British state preferred to defend the Unionist regime and criticize the opposition for unreasonable haste in its demands. In this context the split in the Republican movement, which was formalised in January 1970 with the formation of Provisional Sinn Fein and a Provisional Army Council,[80] was to have increasing significance. The issue over which the split had formally taken place — the proposal, accepted by a majority at the IRA's Convention in December 1969, to end the traditional policy of abstention from the Irish, Stormont and Westminster parliaments — produced very different Northern strategies. The majority current, soon labelled the 'Officials', continued to see the way ahead as that of pressure for a deepening of the reform process. This, whilst it was seen as the basis for a crisis of the Unionist party, was not thought to lead to a crisis of the northern state itself. Rather it appears that the Officials shared with sections of the British ruling class and the opposition at Stormont the hope that increasing divisions in the Unionist party would lead to the eventual splitting of that party into its 'moderate' and right components, and thus to a re-alignment of the party system as a whole.[81] This hope was to be confounded as the government of Chichester Clark made it clear that those in the 'centre' had no intention of giving up the Unionist party's aspiration to a monolithic dominance of the Protestant bloc. In this it was simply continuing O'Neill's strategy of combining reforms with public order measures against the civil rights movement. At the same time, sensing the increasing British exasperation with the reforms' failure to pacify, Chichester Clark proved even less willing than O'Neill to interfere with 'traditional' Orange marches. The result was fierce rioting in North and East Belfast, which saw the first sustained military action by the Provos as a defence force. There were seven Protestant deaths and the resultant intensity of sectarian bitterness led to the expulsion of 500 Catholics from the shipyard.[82]

The split in the republican movement had some of the aspects of a left-right division. When it occurred the Provisionals were extremely critical of 'Communist infiltration', and of attempts to make political alliances with 'extreme socialist' groups.[83] A reading of the memoirs of Sean MacStiofain, Provo chief of staff, makes clear his rigid Catholicism and his ignorant anti-Communism.[84] Whilst these attitudes were to be of great importance for the future evolution and transformation of the Officials, they were, in immediate terms, of less significance. For it is also clear that the split in the republican movement reflected the relationship of traditional republican military struggle tactics to the developing civil rights mobilisations in the north. The collapse of the 1956-62 military campaign had taught the leadership of the Officials that it was the movement's concentration on physical force which had separated it from the masses, and that republicanism should get more directly involved in 'social' issues which reflected the needs of the 'people'. In its reassessment of the situation after 1962, the Republican movement had begun to shed its elitist and politically barren militarism, but it had not yet deepened its analysis of the national question. 'British imperialism' was still defined as the enemy, and it was still held to rule Ireland through a direct colony in the north and a neo-colonial state in the south.[85] It was argued that the British ruling class was now in favour of complete integration of the economies of the two Irish states, and that this was the main reason for divisions in Unionism: 'Unionism led by Captain O'Neill, has been given its instructions by its British masters to make itself more respectable, to brush discrimination, gerrymandering and bigotry under the table.' The failure of militarism demanded 'the development of the anti-imperialist struggle on a new plan — on social and economic issues in the

South and on democratic and civil rights issues in the North.'[86]

There was in fact little that was novel in these arguments. Many of them can be traced back to the divisions in the republican movement in the Thirties which had led to the formation of the leftist Republican Congress.[87] The tiny Irish communist movement had maintained a degree of ideological continuity with these positions and there were close links between it, the British based Connolly Association and the republican 'rethinking' of the sixties.[88] The fact that such influences were anathema to traditionalists like MacStiofain should not however lead us to ignore their own major inadequacies. Central here was the failure to analyse the nature of the Northern state, which was treated as an imperialist imposition relying for its mass basis on encouraging sectarianism amongst the masses. It was therefore assumed that, if the civil rights movement brought about a crisis of the Unionist regime, this would 'set free' Catholic and Protestant workers for progressive politics.[89] The over simplified notion of sectarianism as inculcated from 'above' led to problems for the Officials in their approach to the intensifying crisis of the Unionist state. As it was assumed that partition acquired its basis in sectarianism, the civil rights demands were seen as effectively corrosive of popular support for Unionism and hence ultimately of partition itself.

The inadequacies of the Officials' strategy is often explained in terms of their importation from the communist movement of a 'stages theory.'[90] In fact it is more true to argue that it was precisely the lack of an adequately grounded conception of what the 'stage' of a reformed north would represent that disabled the Officials in their competition with the Provisionals. For once it became clear that the civil rights mobilisation was leading, not to the ideological disintegration of Unionism but rather to its political division and the associated crisis of the state, their continued commitment to the reform of the Stormont regime and opposition to direct rule allowed the Provisionals to represent them as conservatives who had been left behind by events.[91]

There is a curious complicity between references to the Provos as 'Green fascists' funded by Fianna Fail and attempts by their supporters on the left to portray their growth from 1970 on as a simple product of the needs of the Catholic ghettos for protection.[92] For different reasons both approaches necessarily obliterate the types of political calculation which were crucial to the rapid development of the Provisionals in this period.

While it is clear that the conflagration of August 1969 had favoured the growth of a communalist militia amongst the Catholic masses, and that the Provos derived some of their support from Catholic sectarianism, Provisional strategy aimed at integrating this into a wider movement. For this strategy to be successful, Unionism would have to be represented as increasingly crisis ridden, vulnerable but, just because of this, blindly vicious.[93] This representation of Unionism was not simply based on an analysis of existing divisions, for it was hoped that Provo military action would exacerbate the situation. Within four months of the split the Provisionals were involved in a bombing campaign against commercial targets, which often were premises owned by prominent Unionist businessmen. As it was believed that the Catholic masses still tended to favour defensive military activity, these bombings were not claimed.[94] The Provisionals were right to calculate that the bombings, by demonstrating defensive military capacity and by emphasising the existence of 'no-go' areas, would lead to further divisions within Unionism and would force even greater British involvement in Northern Ireland.

The Conservative victory in June and Maudling's appointment as Home Secretary were subsequently blamed by the Labour Party for a rapid deterioration in the situation, through their alleged adoption of a more decidedly pro-Unionist stance. However, crucial decisions like those allowing Orange marches to go ahead and the arms search and curfew in the Lower Falls — which led to gun battles between the Army and both Officials and Provisionals[95] — had been prefigured in the previous government's growing exasperation with the situation and in their tendency to blame it on 'sinister elements' stirring up the Catholic masses.[96] Both Labour and Conservative governments, moreover, had been committed to keeping Chichester Clark in power. As the *Economist* put it in the last months of the Wilson government — 'The British government does not want to take Northern Ireland over. Not Mr Wilson nor Mr Callaghan, not Mr Heath nor Mr Hogg would want to do anything of the kind if they could possibly avoid it.'[97] The only way to avoid intervention was to support Chichester Clark. By the middle of 1970, however, the Unionists were so divided that the British government had no choice but to accept Chichester Clark's concessions to his critics, and to Paisley in particular. The crucial development here was the breakthrough of Paisley's Protestant Unionist Party into Stormont and Westminster politics (Paisley himself was elected for North Antrim in June). Paisley owed his success to the key part he had played organising physical opposition to the civil rights marches. The very divisions in the Unionist Party allowed Paisley to claim the tradition of militant Protestant populism as his own. As well as opposing all reforms, he and his supporters claimed that the increasing social dislocation was a direct product of the government's acquiescence in the dismantling of a distinctively Protestant set of security apparatuses.[98]

With the Provisionals' successful defence of Catholic areas at the end of June, Chichester Clark's position became a very precarious one. He had private discussions with Paisley and the other PUP MP, in which he appeared to take seriously their idea of a new 'peoples militia' to augment the army and RUC.[99] Such talks were clearly designed to undermine potential British government resistance to more repressive legislation, or to 'exemplary' military activity in Catholic areas. The result was the Criminal Justice (Temporary Provisions) Bill, bringing in mandatory six-month minimum prison terms for rioting, and the Falls Road curfew. The idea that such concessions would consolidate support for the regime was wholly chimerical. Divisions in the Unionist party were by now irreconcilable. The post-August reforms had unleashed a very negative dialectic between intra-Unionist division and popular Catholic reaction. The actual and implicit restructuring of the Northern Ireland state pushed Unionist divisions to such a level as to create an atmosphere of fevered uncertainty regarding the whole future of the northern regime. British threats to impose direct rule, if Chichester Clark was overthrown,[100] merely served to shore the regime up, whilst doing nothing to counteract the slide into uncontrollable violence.

The Provo bombing campaign, which continued throughout

the summer of 1970, had not made direct rule inevitable. The reform programme had itself so undermined the traditional functioning of the state that it would very probably have collapsed anyway. Rather the bombing campaign was part of the Provisional strategy of establishing hegemony in Catholic politics. The lack of coherent response on the part of 'constitutional' anti-Unionists (and the Officials) to the crisis of the Unionist state allowed the Provisionals to depict the increasingly beleaguered regime as doomed and in its violent collapse to predict the creation of favourable conditions for the resolution of the 'National question'. By the end of the summer, Chichester Clark had narrowly survived a vote of confidence in his own constituency association and made a further concession by appointing John Taylor, a strident critic of the reform programme, as a minister of state in the Ministry of Home Affairs (the department responsible for the police). The Provisionals predicted that internment would soon occur.[101]

The Provisionals grew in strength by exploiting the contradiction at the heart of the post-1969 reformist strategy. The introduction of the reforms inevitably divided the Unionist party at all levels, yet it was this party, or at least the 'moderate' section of it, which was also charged with continuing to rule the north. Whilst a modernising and reforming Unionist party bereft of state power was a possibility, a Unionist regime with the double responsibility of reforming and reproducing mass support was not. The contradiction was temporarily resolved by a series of concessions to the right and by increasingly strident demands that Heath and Maudling allow the army to adopt a more offensive role, particularly in the 'no-go' areas.

In 1971, for the first time since the beginning of the crisis, Tory backbenchers began to insist that something be done — alarmed by the first Provisional killings, in February and March, of British soldiers — Chichester Clark resigned in March after the government had responded to a series of demands, including military occupation of the 'no-go' areas, with a cosmetic promise of 1,300 extra troops. Maudling and Carrington, the Minister of Defence, came under severe criticism at a meeting of the Home Affairs committee, which was attended by over 160 Tory backbenchers.[102] This expression of visceral support for action against the Provisionals was, however, to have little effect on Heath's attitudes to the formulation of policy on Northern Ireland. His tendency to rely on what one commentator has referred to as 'brazen capitalist rationality . . . and the weakening of the grip of traditional mystification'[103] meant that he approached Northern Ireland with an exaggerated version of the general ruling class tendency to see it as an anachronism which, as far as possible, should be prevented from infecting the rest of the United Kingdom. The advice that he had been receiving from officials who had, since 1969, been more closely involved in monitoring the regime would have been almost uniformly dismissive of the leadership of the Unionist party.[104] Chichester Clark's weak and vacillating leadership had by the time of his resignation, earned him the British government's contempt. Although the resignation was to prompt a lot of speculation about the imminence of direct rule it soon became clear that Heath, with the support of Wilson, was prepared to support Brian Faulkner as a successor.[105] Faulkner had superficially a lot to recommend him to Heath. He was, as even some of his opponents recognised, the only Unionist politician with a degree of professional competence.[106] As an erstwhile supporter of O'Neill put it, without any evident irony, 'Faulkner is faster on his feet, more hard working and more fascinated by politics than any other politician. The comparison with Harold Wilson is irresistible.'[107] Faulkner was able to persuade Heath and Maudling of his substance as a reformist by producing proposals for a new committee system which would integrate the opposition into the Stormont system. He had hoped that such innovations would win the SDLP's support for the policy of internment which, in the wake of the Provisonal bombing campaign of spring 1971, was admitted by Heath to be necessary.[108]

The degree to which the Provisionals were now setting the political agenda was increasingly evident. The bipartisan commitment to the policies of reform through the Unionist regime created the febrile political and ideological conditions in which a bombing campaign was most effective. As importantly, the clear declaration by the Provisionals that they were working for direct rule[109] as a transitional goal, made it all the more difficult for the British ruling class to consider this option — outside of conditions of near catastrophe in Northern Ireland.

NOTES

1. Alan Warde, *Consensus and Beyond: the Development of Labour Party Strategy Since the Second World War* (Manchester 1982) p. 96

2. Bew *et al* p. 153.

3. M Farrell, *Northern Ireland, The Orange State* (London 1976) p.231.

4. P Bew and H Patterson, *Sean Lemass and the Making of Modern Ireland* (Dublin 1982) pp. 195-6

5. Bew *et al* p. 155.

6. Interview with senior Ulster civil servant

7. Bew *et al* p. 120.

8. E Rumpf and A C Hepburn, *Nationalism and Socialism in Twentieth Century Ireland* (Liverpool 1977) p. 202.

9. Northern Ireland's significance was geographic and strategic — the regime signally failed to achieve an impressive popular mobilisation for the anti-fascist struggle. See R Fisk, *In Time of War* (London 1983). For the irritation of Harold Wilson, then a British Civil Servant, on this score, see P Ratcliffe, *Northern Ireland and the Second World War* PRONI Belfast 1977.

10. Bew and Patterson, p. 48.

11. Ibid, p. 49.

12. PRO CP (49) 4 quoted in *Close to Home: Lessons from Ireland*, Troops Out Movement nd p. 38.

13. Bob Purdie, 'The Friends of Ireland' in T Gallagher and J O'Connell eds *Contemporary Irish Studies* (Manchester 1983) p. 84.

14. See Bew and Patterson.

15. Purdie, p. 90.

16. Ian McAllister, 'Political Parties: Traditional and Modern' in J Darby ed. *Northern Ireland: The Background to the Conflict* (Belfast 1983) p. 64.

17. Purdie, p. 62.

18. Bew and Patterson, p. 11.

19. Harold Wilson, *The Labour Government 1964-70* (London 1974) p. 110.

20. *Belfast Newsletter* 5 October 1964

21. *The Labour Government*, p. 140.

22. Bew *et al* chapter 5.

23. Charles Brett, *Long Shadows Cast Before* (London and Edinburgh 1978) p. 135.

24. J H Whyte, 'How much discrimination was there under the Unionist regime, 1921-68?' in *Contemporary Irish Studies* pp. 30-31.

25. Bew *et al* chapters 2 and 3.

26. L O'Dowd, B Rolston and M Tomlinson *Northern Ireland Between Civil Rights and Civil War* (London 1980) p. 12.

27. See Sam McAughtry, 'The Fall of the NILP' in *Irish Times* 19 May 1981.

28. Wilson, p. 843.

29. Farrell, p. 244.

30. Denis Norman, 'Britain's Northern Ireland Policy 1968-70' Unpublished paper.

31. J A Oliver, *Working at Stormont* (Dublin 1978) p. 89.

32. Rumpf and Hepburn, pp. 183-195.

33. In 1968 he was still rejecting greater intervention by arguing that back-benchers should not 'underrate what has been done' House of Commons *Debates* vol 1765, 21 May 1968, col 280

34. Richard Rose's 'Loyalty Questionnaire' in the mid-60s found that Catholics were almost evenly split on the 'constitutional position' of Northern Ireland —

33% approving, 34% disapproving. *Governing without Consensus* (London 1971) p. 477

35. See Sarah Nelson, *Ulster's Uncertain Defenders: Loyalists and the Northern Ireland Conflict* (Belfast 1984) chapter 5.

36. This march was organised by the Peoples Democracy — the student-based activist body which contained, as Michael Farrell puts it, 'a tough Young Socialist hard core' Farrell, p. 247.

37. *Irish Times* 24 April 1970

38. *Irish Times* 2 April 1969

39. *New Left Review* 55, May/June 1969 p. 11

40. Ibid, p. 6.

41. *Irish Times* 22 April 1969

42. *Irish Times* 24 June 1969

43. *Irish Times* 29 April 1969

44. *Irish Times* 2 May 1969

45. Crossman Diaries vol III (London 1977) p. 478.

46. House of Commons *Debates* vol 784, 22 May 1969, col 103

47. *Irish Times* 22 May 1969

48. Sunday Times Insight Team *Ulster*(London 1972) pp. 84-5, 110.

49. Wilson p. 877

50. *Irish Times* 20 August 1969

51. *Irish Times* 30 August 1969, 27 March 1970

52. *Irish Times* 22 August 1969

53. Crossman commented 'Frankly, it is the only successful diplomatic episode in these five years of a Labour government, a one man success story' in G Bell, *Troublesome Business* London 1982 p. 110.

54. *Irish Times* 9 October 1969

55. *Irish Times* 9 October 1969

56. Ibid

57. *Irish Times* 27 March 1970

58. House of Commons *Debates* vol 795, 4 February 1970, col 125

59. See Farrell, p. 272.

60. *Irish Times* 3 and 4 April 1970

61. Thus Austin Currie 'the minority in Northern Ireland were rapidly throwing away the huge amount of international good will which they had earned over the past eighteen months.' *Irish Times* 3 April 1970

62. House of Commons *Debates* vol 799, 7 April 1970, col 318

63. Ibid col 321

64. *Irish Times* 17 April 1970

65. *Irish News* 21 April 1970

66. *Irish Times* 15, 16 June 1970

67. There was fierce rioting in North and East Belfast that resulted in six deaths and the expulsion of 500 Catholics from the Harland and Wolff shipyard *Irish Times* 30 June 1970

68. *Sunday Times* 21 November 1971 and J Downey *Them and Us* (Dublin 1983) p. 60

69. J Callaghan *A House Divided* (London 1973) p. 157

70. *Irish Times* 2 February and 18 February 1970

71. B Rolston 'Reformism and Sectarianism' in Darby pp. 198-99

72. The Home Office view is reflected in interviews Michael McInerney conducted at the time. See *Irish Times* 2 January 1970.

73. Thus Faulkner on the United Kingdom representative 'I felt sure that it

would merely undermine the authority of the Government and provide a channel of complaint by Nationalists . . . ' *Memoirs of a Statesman* (London 1978) p. 65

74. In April the party's annual conference — the Ulster Unionist Council passed a resolution opposing the creation of a central housing body. *Irish News* 25 April 1970

75. *Irish Times* 8 October 1969

76. House of Commons *Debates* vol. 799, 7 April 1970, col 280

77. C Hewitt, 'Catholic grievance, Catholic nationalism and violence in Northern Ireland during the Civil Rights period: a reconsideration' *British Jounal of Sociology* vol 32, No 3, September 1981

78. See Fitt interview with *Irish Times* on formation of SDLP — 22 August 1970 'I think the priority of the party is first of all to bring about a real alternative to the Unionist Party . . . a party which will bring a real live working involvement in the parliamentary institutions of Northern Ireland'.

79. Ibid col 1263

80. K Kelley, *The Longest War: Northern Ireland and the IRA* (London 1982) p. 126.

81. Thus, in the Official's paper, *The United Irishman*, we find the following evaluation of the potential effects of the civil rights movement: 'The movement may thus bring about a completely new polarisation of forces in the six counties — on the one hand, a right wing conservative Unionist group which would undoubtedly draw considerable middle class Catholic support if the alternative should develop from the Civil Rights Movement as a radical socialist grouping . . . ' *United Irishman* December 1968

82. *Irish Times* 30 June 1970

83. Farrell, ibid, p. 270.

84. Sean MacStiofain, *Revolutionary in Ireland* (Farnborough, Hants) 1974 p. 135.

85. *Republican Manual of Education Part 2 1922-66* (Dublin 1972) pp. 21-9

86. Ibid, p. 24.

87. See G Gilmore, *The Republican Congress* (Dublin 1934 reprinted 1966).

88. See M Millotte, *Communism in Modern Ireland* (Dublin and New York) 1984 p. 265.

89. The *United Irishman* attempted to argue that it was the various undemocratic features of the state that prevented the Protestant masses from rallying to the republican movement: '. . . the basic principles of democracy — freedom of speech, assembly and publication were at present flouted in the North and thus made it very difficult for the Republican movement to put across its case for the establishment of a united state and nation in Ireland.' October 1970. This notion of the Protestant masses as essentially misguided, duped 'Irishmen' whilst clearly politically and ideologically more progressive than the view of them as a 'colon' element ripe for expulsion shares its incapacity to analyse the material bases of Unionism.

90. See K Kelly, pp. 88-9.

91. The Provisionals' Belfast paper *Republican News* referred to the Officials as 'Redmonites of the far left . . . coming as it did at a time of fast developing classical revolutionary activity.' September/October 1970. The reference is to John Redmond the leader of the Irish Parliamentary Party at the time of the First World War who supported the British war effort.

92. See G Bell, *The British in Ireland* (London 1984) p. 46. It is clear, however, that the division of the republican movement into 'left' and 'right' factions was a long-standing objective of the Irish state. See 'The Berry Papers' *Magill* June 1980

93. *Republican News* August 1970: 'Stormont and the Unionist Party are on the

run and beaten, but remember . . . the last kick of a dying regime is usually the worst and most vicious.'

94. Kelly, p. 138.

95. Farrell, p. 273.

96. See speech by Roy Hattersley *Irish News* on 4 April 1970

97. *Economist* 16 May 1970

98. C Smyth, *The Ulster Democratic Unionist Party* PhD Queens University Belfast, 1983 p. 28.

99. *Irish Times* 2 July 1970

100. *Irish Times* 11 August 1970

101. See *Republican News* September/October 1970

102. P Norton *Conservative Dissidents* (London 1978) p. 50

103. R Blackburn, 'The Heath Government' *New Left Review* 70, November/December 1970 p. 23.

104. One senior Home Office Official is credited with commenting on O'Neill and his cabinet 'None can be trusted, all are second rate.' See A Verrier, *Through the Looking Glass* (London 1983) p. 293.

105. See article by Peter Jenkins *Guardian* 22 March 1971

106. See Charles Brett's clear preference for him over O'Neill in *Long Shadows Cast Before* p. 135 and *New Statesman* editorial 26 March 1971

107. John Cole *Guardian* 22 March 1971

108. See debate on internment House of Commons *Debates* vol 823, 22 September 1971, col 3

109. *Republican News*, a substantial piece on the implications of direct rule.

2

From Internment to the Ulster Workers' Council Strike: Emergence of a Strategy

In 1971 there had been prior to internment (9 August), thirty four deaths in the North; between internment and the end of the year there were 139.[1] Though Heath and Maudling were still declaring in early 1972 that 'terrorism' would have to be defeated before any political initiative could succeed,[2] the disastrous decision to introduce internment did lead to a reconsideration of ruling-class strategy towards the north. The intensity of the Provisionals' response to internment made it difficult to consider openly direct rule — the interim objective for which they were waging their campaign and, after internment, the demand of the southern government as well.[3] However, a survey of the discussion which increasingly did take place within the ruling class does reveal two lines of argument. The most obvious was an increasing tendency to talk in terms of the 'ultimate' need for withdrawal, since the failure of the reform programme was taken to illustrate the essential futility of attempting to provide 'English', that is, 'reasonable' solutions for the 'Irish' those essentially 'unreasonable' people. These considerations of withdrawal were nevertheless carefully modulated. Thus, the *Spectator*, referring to the government's professed intention of securing military pacification as a prelude to any political movement as 'foolish stuff', went on to praise Wilson's recent plan for an Irish settlement (see below) for broaching the question of withdrawal:

> There is no disposition in England to hang on to any part of Ireland, and what would best suit the British government and

> British opinion would be for a change of mind to take place whereby the majority in Northern Ireland became prepared seriously to consider the conditions under which the unification of Ireland could be made acceptable.[4]

At the same time it insisted that 'any unification without the consent of the northern majority would risk spreading over all Ireland the mess which is now chiefly confined in the north.' The southern state would have to prove itself by public acceptance of the need for northern majority consent and by joint anti-IRA actions with the British state. It would also have to participate in a Constitutional Commission with the object of creating a secular constitution for a new Irish state. The catalyst in developing this approach was Wilson. In November, after a visit to the Republic and the North, he put forward his 'Fifteen Point Plan' for a solution. The central proposition was that the effects of internment on Catholic politics determined the need for a new response from the British state.

> I believe that the situation has now gone so far that it is impossible to conceive of an effective long term solution which is not in some way directed to finding a means of achieving the aspiration towards a United Ireland . . . . A substantial term of years will be required before any concept of unification could become a reality but the dream must be there. If men of moderation have nothing to hope for, men of violence will have something to shoot for.[5]

The progress towards a united Ireland would have to be based on Protestant consent and it is in this area that the superficial nature of the new strategy was most obvious. There was no attempt to explain why it was thought likely that the consent of a substantial proportion of the Protestant population would be forthcoming for reunification, even if it were implemented gradually, over a period of fifteen or more years, as Wilson proposed. However, the continuation of the process of division and redivision in Protestant politics did give rise to a degree of desperate optimism in some ruling-class circles. The increasingly eccentric trajectory of Paisleyism was of crucial importance here. Identified, when elected to Westminster in April 1970, as the embodiment of Protestant reaction and primitivism, Paisley subsequently began to modify the purely negative character of his movement. In August 1971 he opposed internment, on the grounds that the government would intern as many Protestants as Catholics. In October he proclaimed the imminence of direct rule and declared his support for the full integration of Northern Ireland into the United Kingdom. On southern radio he even speculated on the positive effects the secularisation of the Republic's constitution would have on Protestant attitudes to a United Ireland. The Provisional leader David O'Connell described the Paisleyites as 'allies in the cause of a new Ireland.'

The crisis of the Unionist party, inasmuch as it made the emergence of a serious oppositional force in Protestant politics seem increasingly feasible, was responsible for these changes in Paisley's politics. At first Paisley had considered the possibility of an alliance with Craig, and with those sections of the Unionist Party which had opposed the reform programme. Negotiations for the formation of a new party took place in 1971 but collapsed, largely because the right in the Unionist Party believed that it was still possible to recapture it. As a result, in September 1971 Paisley and the socially radical Unionist dissident, Desmond Boal, announced the formation of the Democratic Unionist Party which was to 'be on the right on constitutional issues and on the left on social issues.'[6] The alliance with Boal represented a realisation on Paisley's part that his political base was too narrow to provide an effective challenge to Unionism. It was still heavily dependent on evangelical Protestants living by and large in the rural areas, many of whom were mobilised through his own Free Presbyterian church. The formation of the DUP, the alliance with Boal and the associated emphasis, at least in the rhetoric, on social radicalism, was aimed at expanding the party's support in Belfast. The support for direct rule and integration was purely opportunist. Paisley quite correctly calculated that direct rule would be a body blow to the Unionist party, robbing it of control of the local state apparatus.

The split in what had been seen as a monolithic Protestant right meant that the conditions for some sort of radical initiative appeared to exist. But this was only so because — as was clear from Wilson's plan — such calculations were based on the transparently arrogant and ill-formed assumption that the British state was capable of manipulating the major political forces in both Irish states. Thus Wilson, whilst continuing to oppose direct rule, proposed that the existing Unionist regime agree both to Catholic participation in government and to a transfer of security powers to Westminster[7] — demands which the Faulkner regime could never have accepted without losing all popular support. At the same time the British recognition of the necessity of eventual re-unification was supposed to ensure the rapid transfer of Catholic support from the Provos to the SDLP, and thus allow them to enter a coalition with the Unionists and have the support of the southern government.

The response of the political parties in the south was a predictable one. Lynch described the plan as 'highly important', though both Fianna Fail and Fine Gael rejected Wilson's exotic suggestion that the Republic should rejoin the Commonwealth.[8] Heath in an earlier speech had referred to Catholic desires for unity as legitimate and this, combined with the Wilson speech, led many to believe that the terms of the Irish debate had been qualitatively altered.[9] The leaders of both parties clearly shared a desire to be rid of an increasingly embarrassing set of commitments; their aspirations were, in this sense, the same. As the *Economist* put it at the beginning of 1972: 'Ministers have made little secret of their belief that the most satisfactory solution in the end would be if a political solution were created over the years in which the Protestant majority in the north could come to recognise a future for itself in a united Ireland.'[10] However, there is no evidence that Heath was willing to accept Wilson's central thesis that the British state should accept unification as an object of policy. Heath had no record of previous interest in Northern Ireland or in the Irish question. More importantly, unlike Wilson, — the failure of whose grander plans for the modernisation of Britain lent a desperate attractiveness to any 'solution' to the Irish question — Heath's commitment to radical foreign and domestic policies[11] led him to see Northern Ireland as an avoidable distraction. By allowing Faulkner, Maudling and the army to deal with it he showed that for the first eighteen months of his government he did not have a policy. Certainly, in terms of his own governmental ideology, presiding over the Faulkner regime was not what was understood as implementing a serious policy.

The decision to implement Direct Rule had nothing to do with any desire on Heath's part to re-open and resolve the Irish question. Impelled by the fear that the identification of the British role in the north with rampant militarism was damaging the state's reputation in Europe, he cut through the tangle of constitution-mongering which had preoccupied the cabinet's Northern Ireland committee. In line with his approach to the introduction of new policies — particularly the U-turns on economic and trade union policy, the influences on him were extra-parliamentary and extra-cabinet — in this case the Central Policy Review Staff.[12] Faulkner had been allowed to stay in power, not as was so often speculated at the time, because of fears that radical initiatives would split the Tory party or provoke a Protestant backlash, but rather because of the lack of any serious and convincing alternative. Certainly Wilson's plan was less than convincing in its attempts to combine commitment to ultimate withdrawal with Protestant consent. The very insulation of Northern Ireland from the rest of the United Kingdom's political system also meant that it was impossible for even informed speculation about possible Protestant responses to direct rule or other initiatives to take place. The Unionist regime and all Unionist politicians were now completely discredited and there is little evidence that the members of the SDLP were held in much more respect.[13] The one source of information which had existed and been developed since 1969 was the link between the Home Office and the Northern Ireland Civil Service, which was now supplemented by the United Kingdom representative and the Army. The information that did exist tended to reinforce reluctance to get more involved.

Nowhere was this more clear than in a substantial analysis of the implications of direct rule by Richard Rose, the one British-based academic to have taken a serious interest in Ulster in the previous decade. A considerable amount of the analysis was given over to speculation on various scenarios which would necessitate the abolition of the Unionist regime and possible forms of Catholic and Protestant reaction. His prognosis was a bleak one:

> Realistically, the best response that London might hope for is a short, intense and totally unsuccessful attack from indigenous opponents, an attack that can be repressed by the British army

with no civilian casualties. At worst, London faces the prospect of a majority of Protestants and a majority of Catholics opposing the new regime by massive displays of defiance and violence . . . before deciding to suspend Stormont they would be well advised to consider that the long term situation could get worse instead of better in consequence of their actions.[14]

This rather measured pessimism did not prevent Rose from providing a serious attempt to sketch out the institutional and political ramifications of direct rule. He pointed out that removing the political superstructure of the Unionist regime would not be disabling to the actual government of the province: 'the substantial administrative apparatus of Stormont, would remain intact. Westminster would inherit a working system of government.' Executive authority would now reside in a British minister of cabinet rank. He would be advised by a 'council of Ulster residents' who could have assigned to them specific departmental obligations. Rose's only concession to those who might question the colonialist flavour of his proposals was to stipulate that the members of the council should be drawn from the ranks of Unionist and opposition politicians. He made it clear that ruling-class thinking was unsympathetic to the north's politicians — 'London would dearly love to be shed of all elective politicians in Ulster.' But, as he pointed out, the use of non-political advisers 'would be to deny the successor regime any hope of support from established political organisations.' At the same time Rose evidently saw the function of local politicians under a direct rule regime as being little more than that of giving advice and mobilising support for the new regime.

The importance of Rose's analysis consisted less in what it said than in what it did not say. There was absolutely no attempt to depict direct rule as in any sense a stage to some 'final solution'. This analysis therefore contemplated the abolition of the Stormont regime from what was still essentially a Unionist position. Although it was produced before the introduction of internment there is no reason to think that its essential elements were in any way transformed by that development. Rose's analysis is of major significance. For it clearly delineated a relatively radical strategy towards the Unionist regime which was in no sense dependent upon a reappraisal of the constitutional relationship between Britain and the North. Since those who proposed it had no confidence that it would succeed, there was little likelihood of its being introduced except in circumstances of intense turmoil in the north. This was to have the consequence of obscuring its very existence. The inevitable result was the generation of endless illusions about the dimensions of Heath's Northern Ireland policy.

What was the basis for this alternative strategy in Northern Ireland? Despite the emphasis in the public statements of British ministers on the good relations they had with the Northern Ireland Civil Service[15] — and the high calibre of its higher ranks there — direct rule was to mean a radical restructuring of the state's administration. As we have demonstrated elsewhere,[16] the NICS was one of the main areas where the Unionist regime had systematically chosen to demonstrate its 'Protestant' character. Whilst there was no direct attempt to deal with the lack of Catholic representation in the higher reaches of the administration,[17] the creation of a new ministry — the Northern Ireland Office (NIO) — to service the Secretary of State, was to be the basis on which the main lines of functioning of the main apparatuses were to be redrawn. As various critics of the NICS had noted, despite the relatively small size of the bureaucracy there was surprisingly poor communication and co-ordination between departments.[18] The problem was not an administrative one; rather, it reflected the exigencies of the predominant Unionist political strategy of populism, which dictated that the state apparatuses be responsive to their clienteles. It was just this sort of responsiveness that the re-organisation brought about by the creation of the NIO was to bring to an end. The NIO was to become the effective apex and co-ordinator of the whole administrative machine and, although most of the Stormont departments continued to exist,[19] their interrelations and varying degrees of autonomy were transformed. Although it was at first necessary to rely upon some of the main personnel from the old regime,[20] their new role was clearly to be a subordinate one. Indeed, the great majority of the 'policy' group within the NIO — those responsible for the main lines of policy development under the new regime — were United Kingdom civil servants on secondment.[21] In this manner an administrative apparatus was created which, in its mode of operation, was heavily dependent upon Westminster and Whitehall.

Such a strategy, by tightening the links between the Northern state apparatus and the central state, would inevitably have the effect either of relegating local political organisations to the role of opposition or, as Rose fondly hoped, of delivering the support of the masses to the new system of government. Naturally the logic of this development could not be openly avowed, precisely because it was most likely to unify the blocs in opposition. Thus it was the proclaimed objective of the new regime to create the conditions for its own supersession. Direct Rule was only a 'temporary measure',[22] which was supposed to create the conditions for a new type of political accommodation in the north. However, it was made clear that this regime would not be allowed to forget its strict subordination to Westminster. As the government's White Paper put it: 'Any new institutions must be of a simple and businesslike character appropriate to the powers and functions of a local authority.'[23] The cutting down of power and pretensions was also clearly designed to make some form of power-sharing arrangement between Unionist and Nationalists easier by ensuring that the only 'powers' to be shared were limited and non-controversial.

Though it was recognised that the abolition of Stormont would be seen as a victory for Catholics, it was thought that Protestants could be reassured by the guarantee that there would be no change in the 'constitutional position' without the consent of a majority of the population in the north. Those Protestants who remained recalcitrant would be reminded of the extent of Britain's financial commitment to the province. Thus, in a Commons debate just after a Vanguard strike against direct rule (see below), the new Secretary of State for Northern Ireland, William Whitelaw, whilst expressing a degree of sympathy for the feeling of Protestants outraged by the effects of IRA bombings and the shock of losing 'their' parliament, immediately followed this with a clear reminder of their material dependence on Britain: 'It is important when considering these facts to remember what this country . . . . has provided, not only in terms of our troops, but in other ways, for the Northern Ireland economy. Since 1970 we have given extra financial support which overall represents an additional £100 per head of population.'[24] However the existence of calculations of this sort and, indeed, of any type of strategic thinking, was particularly difficult to decipher in the period after direct rule, since the new regime appeared to be simply responding to an intensifying crescendo of Provisional and Protestant violence.

The Provisionals

Direct rule presented the Provisionals with severe problems. For them it was merely a stage in creating conditions for a final (intensified) struggle to force the British state into serious negotiations. Early in 1972 they had begun to use car bombs, with the objective of 'striking at the colonial economic structure' and making the governance of the North too expensive for Britain.[25] However, even before direct rule, the horrifyingly indiscriminate effects of this weapon[26] were damaging support for the Provisionals who, with characteristic insouciance, expected the state to ensure that streets were cleared of potential civilian casualties. Direct rule itself was clearly seen by the Catholic masses as a major victory which also demanded an end to the military campaign to allow political negotiations to take place in what was seen to be a new set of political conditions which had altered radically in their favour. The SDLP, which had maintained its position of not talking to the British government until internment was ended, now demanded that the Provos declare a ceasefire. Even in strong Provisional areas, such as Belfast's Andersonstown, this period was to see the emergence of local 'peace' group linked to the Catholic church.[27] Some rank and file Provisionals, particularly in the north, saw direct rule as a watershed and favoured a truce.[28] It was not so much mindless militarism which led the Army Council of the IRA and the chief of staff, MacStiofain, to reject this option, but rather an acute fear of losing the initiative to the SDLP.[29] If a truce was to be declared then it would have to be on terms which the Provisionals could represent as a clear step towards their ultimate objectives.

These had been spelt out in September 1971 in a set of constitutional proposals produced by the Provisional Army Council.

The central notion was that of the Dail Uladh (Irish for Ulster Assembly), which was designed to demonstrate the Provisional's concern for Protestant susceptibilities.

> No compromise can be made on the basic quest for an independent 32 county Irish Republic. But it is equally true that Protestant and Unionist fears of being swamped in the Republic must be considered. Their fears could be adequately satisfied if they formed a large part, possibly a majority in an Ulster regional parliament.[30]

This, the most 'advanced' form of Provisional conciliation towards the Unionists, shows how little the republicans understood this crucial issue. Regarding all divisions between 'Irish men' as a product of Britain's interference, they believed that a British declaration of intent to withdraw would remove the active cause of division and that the Unionists would then be amenable to negotiations.[31] This facile optimism was increasingly at odds with the actual conditions in the north where, whilst Unionist political organisations were divided and demoralised, the paramilitary vigilantism of the Ulster Defence Association was mobilising tens of thousands of petty-bourgeois and working-class Protestants and — most divisive of all — a campaign of sectarian assassinations of Catholics had begun. The incongruities of the Provisionals' position soon became blatantly clear. Thus David O'Connell, vice president of Sinn Fein and an architect of the Dail Uladh programme, visited the Creggan housing estate in Derry and gave a press conference alongside the leader of the local IRA at which he raised the question of direct talks with Protestant 'leaders.'[32] A month later, as sectarian confrontations increased in Belfast, some Provisionals began to get directly involved in attacking Protestants.[33] The rhetoric of a non-sectarian accommodation between Protestants and Catholics was belied by the nature of the Provisional presence in Belfast, which increasingly had the aspect of a communalist army. This contradiction was but one indication of the fact that the Provisonals' period of hegemony in Catholic politics was coming to an end.

Nevertheless they were still firmly emplaced in the predominantly Catholic parts of the North and were quite capable of carrying on their campaign. Whitelaw tried at first to use the Provisionals' manifest political weaknesses to undermine their militiary capacity. The British state — and here we must use an extended definition of the state, which would include the leadership of the Labour party and certain newspapers (the *Times* in particular) — began to work on the weakest link of the Provisionals, namely, their tendency to see direct rule as creating a degree of constitutional fluidity similar to that which had existed in the closing stages of the War of Independence (1918-21). As an article on direct rule put it '(direct rule) places us in a somewhat similar position to that prior to the setting up of Partition and the two statelets. It puts the 'Irish Question' in its true perspective — an alien power seeking to lay claim to a country for which it has no legal right.'[34] In an anticipatory euphoria about direct rule, the Provisionals had proclaimed that 1972 would the 'The Year of Victory.'[35] They desperately needed signs of British ruling-class interest in negotiating. In March Wilson had visited Dublin and met O'Connell and Joe Cahill, a leading Belfast Provisional. On his return the Labour Party for the first time broke with bipartisanship on Ulster by criticising the government's failure to announce an initiative. Wilson made it clear that he favoured the calling of an all-party conference, including the Provisionals.[36]

The Provisionals were coming under increasing pressure to declare a ceasefire. Whitelaw had decided, for tactical reasons, to allow only a minimal army presence in Catholic areas and this, together with the refusal to accede to Unionist demands for the 're-occupation' of the 'No-Go' areas and the selective release of internees,[37] accentuated such pressure. The SDLP, sensing a change of popular mood, felt able to call on all Catholic councillors, magistrates and members of statutory bodies to resume public office.[39] A peace petition circulating in West Belfast had 63,000 signatures by early June.[39] At this time, and in obvious response to these developments. MacStiofain invited Whitelaw to go to Derry to discuss Provisional demands.[40] Although, predictably enough, the demand was publicly rejected, clandestine negotiations were soon under way with the Provisionals, using leading members of the SDLP as initial intermediaries. Whitelaw acted quickly to demonstrate the supposed seriousness of British interest by granting political status to 120 Provisional prisoners, some of whom were on hunger strike, and releasing from detention Gerry Adams, a leading Belfast IRA man.[41] Adams and O'Connell negotiated directly with the most senior officials in the NIO, and the Provisionals, obviously impressed with the status which appeared to have been accorded to them, agreed to an indefinite truce.[42] The only conditions appear to have been an end to all Army activity in Catholic areas and a promise that, if the truce held for a reasonable period, the Provisionals would meet Whitelaw for direct negotiations.

Even before the truce was declared, the process of 'dealing' with the Provisionals had begun in earnest. Whitelaw had announced in parliament plans for a conference on the political future of the north to which 'all shades of opinion' were to be invited.[43] A *Times* leader speculated as to whether the Provisionals might be invited. After the declaration of the truce, the same newspaper claimed that the Provisionals' failure to insist on an end to internment or a British declaration of intent to withdraw as preconditions were 'facts of the greatest significance.'[44] As the truce continued, the *Times* began to acknowledge the political intelligence of the Provisional leadership:

> The Provisionals, who are now under able political leadership are bent upon having a say in any Northern Ireland settlement proportionate to their power. And that power has not been extinguished. The concessions that Mr Whitelaw is making to the IRA in particular and the Catholic community in general are not yet complete.[45]

However, despite a certain tactical flexibility, the Provisionals were in no way prepared to alter their main demands, as Whitelaw was to discover when he had six of their leadership secretly flown to England for a meeting with him in early July.[46] Even after the subsequent breakdown of the truce and the Provisionals' exposure of the meeting, the British reaction was to still hold out hope that the negotiations could be restarted and to praise the supposed political acumen of some of the Provisional leadership.[47]

This response was in part based on the evidence that even the most intransigent Provos were aware of the dangers of the simple continuation of a military campaign barren of any political perspective.[48] More importantly, it was calculated that the more politicised section of the leadership would ultimately be more flexible in negotiations than the 'militarist' element, usually identified as MacStiofain and Seamus Twomey, who had become Provo Commanders in Belfast after internment. Particularly high hopes were held of O'Connell. Wilson had been impressed by him and even after the breakdown of the truce the *Financial Times* could report that 'some ministers were not too depressed by the attitude displayed by the team's leader, O'Connell. They also see Rory O'Brady and even Joe Cahill as possible "men of reason" '[49] There is some evidence that such expressions of esteem did have an effect on O'Connell.[50] But if the NIO and other opponents of the Provos hoped that there was the basis for a split between politicians and militarists,[51] this simply displayed a mixture of wishful thinking and an incapacity to understand the dynamics of republicanism as an ideology. The differences between O'Connell and MacStiofain, though real, were not such as to threaten a real rupture in that ideology. To argue that the military campaign itself would not successfully dislodge Britain was no doubt correct but the political programme — Dail Uladh/Eire Nua[52] — which O'Connell and O'Brady were particularly associated with, in an important sense simply compounded the problems faced by an ideology which had at its centre the denial that there was any serious *internal* obstacle to the realisation of a 32 county state. Whitelaw, like his successors, was able to 'discover' facets of politics and ideology in the north which were only novel because of the abysmal ignorance of the British ruling-class about even modern (post-1916) Irish history. The hope that the 'concessions' to Protestants envisaged by people like O'Connell represented the germs of a more reasonable republicanism was impossibly utopian. Despite his differences with MacStiofain, O'Connell still accepted the cardinal republican notion that it was the British state which alone could precipitate the re-orientation of Protestant attitudes which was required if the Provisionals' proposals were to be taken seriously.

This tragi-comedy of British attempts to politicize and split the Provos soon reached its *dénouement*. Wilson, who still appears to

have been desperately eager to salvage some claim to states-
manship from his interventions in Ireland, had another meeting
with the Provos in Dublin soon after the collapse of the truce,
when an attempt to rehouse Catholics in a disputed area led to
direct conflict with the British Army. He informed Heath that
there were serious divisions in the movement and that the
chances of a renewed truce were high.[53] The next day the Provos
exploded 20 huge bombs in Belfast killing eleven and injuring
130. Within days there were 4,000 extra troops in the North (a
total of 21,000) and Whitelaw, in a military exercise known as
Operation Motorman, sanctioned the military re-occupation of
the 'No-Go' areas.[54]

Constitutional Nationalism and the Irish Dimension

In an exchange after internment Wilson had criticised Heath for
not realising that Lynch was Britain's 'best Irish Prime
Minister.'[55] Since the onset of the 'Troubles' Lynch had insisted
on the Republic's role as a sort of external representative of the
North's Catholics and predictably reiterated the nationalist
nostrum that unity was the only real solution. However in
substance his policy on the north was to try — largely unsuccessfully from 1969-1972 — to pressure the British state into a
radical reconstruction of the regime in Ulster. He had successfully weathered the 'Arms Crisis' in 1970 — the culmination of a
period when a dissident 'republican' faction in his cabinet,
which had pushed for a more aggressive role towards the North,
had been involved in the clandestine attempts to import guns for
use by the Provisionals in Ulster.[56]

Even in one of the coldest periods of Anglo-Irish relations, in
the months after internment, Lynch had made it clear to Heath
that any radical action by him in the north would produce strong
repression of the Provisionals in the Republic.[57] After direct rule
Lynch was less than happy with the SDLP's refusal to get involved
in direct negotiations with Whitelaw. The ruling class in the
Republic was almost uniformly horrified by Whitelaw's negotiations with the Provos and, after Motorman, Lynch made the
dramatic gesture of sending a helicopter north to bring SDLP

leaders to Dublin, to impress on them the need for a more positive response to Britain.[58] However, the party maintained its position and instead of agreeing to participate in the conference which Whitelaw was planning for late September, published its first substantial policy document — 'Towards a New Ireland.' This advocated a British declaration of intent to withdraw and, as an interim measure, a provincial government based on a coalition of Unionists and Nationalists which would be subordinate not to Westminster but to a joint British-Irish condominium.[59] This put the party in a more stridently anti-partitionist position than Lynch's government, which had already made it clear that it did not want representation in the talks and favoured the main lines of Whitelaw's policy.[60]

When the British Green Paper was published, at the end of October, the basic nature of the new regime, and its place in any restructuring of the existing Anglo-Irish nexus, had become clear. Despite this the southern response was almost pathetically grateful. The government claimed that it represented a 'fantastic advance' and the *Irish Times* political correspondent hailed it as a 'big victory for the North's minority and a big step towards co-operation and ultimate unity.'[61] Such southern euphoria was based on that part of the document — the so-called 'Irish Dimension' — which stated amongst other things that: 'Whatever arrangements are made for the future of Northern Ireland must take into account the Province's relationship with the Republic of Ireland.'[62] In the Commons debate on the document, however, it was clear that southern evaluations were wildly optimistic. Whitelaw in his speech, did little more than emphasise the degree to which any 'solution' would have to involve 'meaningful responsibility in Northern Ireland.' The 'minority' were to be able to 'participate in the running of their own country' and the 'majority' would benefit, as 'Henceforward Northern Ireland would have a constitution which all the people in the country would be prepared to operate . . . .'[63] The 'Irish Dimension' was defended in terms of the benefits for any new regime of Irish government support and action against the IRA. Even a vociferous critic of direct rule like Julian Critchley was moved to defend the conservative advantages of the Irish Dimension: 'The Irish Dimension exists, it is a fact of life which we must acknowledge and accept. Mr Lynch's attitude to the IRA in the south . . .is the key to the eventual military victory for which the security forces are working in the north.'[64]

Such euphoria in the south made it easier for Lynch to increase his anti-Provisional activity. The headquarters of Provisional Sinn Fein were shut down and more and more prominent Provisionals were arrested. At the end of November the government dismissed the entire governing body of the state's television service after the broadcasting, contrary to a government directive, of an interview with MacStiofain.[65] It was clear that the predominant sections of the southern ruling class, whilst not prepared to challenge openly anti-partitionist shibboleths, were less than anxious to get directly involved in the north. 1972 had revealed the horrible potentialities of a military conflict intertwined with massive sectarian violence. The north was thus seen as a miasma of unpredictable elements, so that the southern ruling-class, keen to keep its distance, gladly left the British state with the task of imposing order.[66] Whilst the SDLP were under strong southern pressure to try and work out some accommodation with at least sections of the Unionist population through Whitelaw's mediation, they could not afford to under-estimate the degree to which, although the Provos had lost popular support, their own potential support base would be affected by a too obvious willingness to go along with Whitelaw's plans. For although the Provisionals were weakened politically and had suffered severe losses militarily after 'Motorman', they were far from defeated.[67] More importantly, the original Whitelaw tactic of controlling army activity in Catholic areas, so as to divide the masses from the Provisionals, was abandoned after Motorman. Provisional strongholds were densely occupied by the army — in the greater Andersonstown area it established 17 fortified positions, including three huge corrugated iron forts. It also occupied two schools, the grounds of a college of education and two football stadiums.[68]

The continuation of internment and detention, the dense army presence and the incapacity of the state to control sectarian assassinations combined to produce rather conditional support for the SDLP amongst the Catholic masses. The effect of the post-68 mobilisations had been to create a whole range of local defence groups, community associations and smaller leftish and republican groups which, together with the Provisionals, unceasingly criticised the SDLP and argued that it would shortly be absorbed and coopted.[69]

The weakness of SDLP politics throughout this period was evident not only in relation to its position on internment — it had at least now started to talk to the NIO, although it had originally pledged not to do so until internment was ended[70] — but also in its relative disregard, in terms of policy, for the army presence and its effects. In fact, throughout the period up to the Sunningdale agreement, the party made no attempt to develop a policy on this question; it merely expressed Catholic grievances over particular instances of army behaviour. It is here that one of the main ironies of SDLP's nationalism is most evident. For it was precisely because the party treated direct rule as an antechamber to fundamental constitutional changes that it was able to regard army activity as a problem that would be resolved in passing, as it were, as part of a wider 'solution'. If the SDLP had arrived at a realistic understanding of the possibilites created by direct rule, it would have been forced to adopt a more genuinely critical and intelligent line on the army. Instead, the leadership of the party got involved in fruitless talks with William Craig and John Taylor, two of the most intransigent Unionist opponents of direct rule. Taylor, who was still in the Unionist party, and Craig, as leader of the Vanguard movement, had publicly supported notions of a UDI — movement towards some sort of independent Ulster state to avoid 'Westminster' dictation. However the possibilities of accommodation were slight given that a predominant section of Craig's Vanguard movement saw independence as a means of restoring traditional forms of Protestant domination whilst Taylor insisted that independence would have to be in a British context, 'one which was still loyal to the Queen.'[71] Here the SDLP was simply adopting arguments which had long been common among Irish nationalists, and which were founded upon the false understanding that the anti-British attitudes of Protestants could provide a basis for an accommodation with nationalism.

The SDLP's basic position after direct rule was summed up by one of its leaders in October 1973: 'We have insisted all along that the only long term solution is in the context of Irish reunification. Any short term solution should be set in that direction.'[72] Such views were predominant amongst constitutional nationalists in the north and were clearly articulated in the leader columns of the Catholic daily paper.[73] The existence of severe divisions within Unionism was simply interpreted as an indication of its fundamental weakness and of its inability to resist. Such views were not new. They reflected a very traditional nationalist perspective: that partition was not based on substantial and real divisions in Ireland but on elite manipulation of popular Protestant prejudices. The implication was clear — if the Protestant political elite was deprived of its control of the local state its capacity to mobilise the masses would be severely damaged and movement towards reunification would be relatively smooth. From the constitutional nationalists of the SDLP to the Provisionals there was a consistent tendency to ignore the possibility of a substantial and relatively autonomous, Protestant mass response to anything construed as anti-partitionist.

The SDLP's position was not, of course, determined by ideological factors alone. It also clearly reflected the increasing difficulty with which it maintained its original radical position on internment. Since Motorman there had been an increase in the number of people interned and detained, and the SDLP was under continuous attack from Provisionals, Officials and the PD for continuing to talk with Whitelaw under such conditions.[74] The party had declared that it would participate in the local government elections and later, in the crucial elections for the Northern Ireland Assembly, which the British White Paper of March 1973 had proposed as the first step towards the creation of a new structure of government. The SDLP justified this by arguing that their victory as the main representatives of the north's Catholics would have dramatic effects on British policy and would lead to a quick ending of internment.[75]

The Assembly election results in June 1973 demonstrated the strength of the SDLP. It won 22% of the total vote, brushing aside the Provisional/PD campaign in favour of a boycott of the election, and effectively establishing itself as the official voice of the northern minority.[76] In contrast, the section of the Unionist party led by Faulkner which had reluctantly accepted the White Paper got less support (29%) than the various anti-White Paper unionists (31%). The centre parties, in which the NIO had at first placed so much hope, only won 12% of the total vote between them, with the Alliance party merely drawing support away from the NILP.[77]

The elections took place three months after a general election in the Republic had seen the defeat of Fianna Fail (for the first time since 1954) and the return of a Coalition government of Fine Gael and the small Irish Labour Party. Fine Gael, although formally committed to a united Ireland, was at least as concerned as Lynch had been to ensure that, in the foreseeable future, British energies were expended in reforming the northern regime and not in putting unity on the agenda. Although there was a substantial segment of the Labour Party sympathetic to republicanism, the leadership of the party favoured the reformist position, and the party's Northern Ireland spokesperson, Conor Cruise O'Brien, was an outspoken anti-republican. Certainly the Coalition's public posture contained none of the rather formalistic Fianna Fail demands for a declaration of intent — its election manifesto had emphasised the need 'to promote a peaceful solution in the north' and concentrated on the notion of some form of power-sharing regime.[78] In office, the speeches of the Fine Gael leader and prime minister, Liam Cosgrove, emphasised the need for gradualism. He even went so far as to tell a Conservative meeting in London that any pressure for movement on the issue of partition 'would dangerously exacerbate tension and fears.'[79]

Such views were greeted with consternation and anger in the SDLP. It felt that they would seriously damage its hopes of creating a pan-nationalist united front which would exert irresistible pressure on the British. The focus of disagreement became the very different interpretations which the party and the Coalition wished to put on the Council of Ireland provisions, in the British White Paper's section on the 'Irish Dimension.' This section had been implicitly mimimalist and had envisaged the Council as a body which would have a role in the co-ordination of 'matters of substantial mutual interest.'[80] But it was made clear that this phrase referred to areas such as tourism, regional development and transport, and also that the Council could only be developed 'with the consent of both majority and minority opinion in Northern Ireland.'

From the elections of June 1973 to the autumn of that same year, the NIO did all it could to provide a coherent basis for a coalition government, the basic elements of which would be the Faulkner Unionists, the Alliance Party and the SDLP. The British government and the Coalition government in Ireland were initially agreed that the SDLP should participate in a reconstructed northern regime, with a weak Council of Ireland serving to express the 'Irish Dimension.' By the end of the summer, however, the SDLP had forced the Coalition into a complete *volte face*.

A large number of SDLP delegations visited the south in this period, hoping to convince the leaders of the Coalition that their position was undermining SDLP negotiating strength with the British.[81] These visits were to prove remarkably successful. In early September, John Hume and other party leaders had a series of discussions with Cosgrave and Corish, the leader of the Labour Party, which eliminated any significant differences of approach.[82] Later that month, Hume and others attended a one day meeting on the question of a Council of Ireland, where they compared draft proposals with Irish government officials. Hume was later able to tell the Assembly party that 'they (the drafts on a Council of Ireland) were found to be substantially similar and would be stressed strongly during the Heath — Cosgrave talks. . . '[83] There had been a radical change in Irish government policy. The Coalition government now supported the SDLP's notion of a Council of Ireland with substantial powers; it would also make it clear that the whole complex of new institutions was intended to be a transitional stage on the way to unity.

Without full access to official papers we can only speculate as to the reasons for the change in the Coalition's position. It was certainly the case that the SDLP's substantial electoral victory had increased its self confidence and it was also quite well aware that the irredentism of the Republic's official ideology made it difficult for a southern government to be in open disagreement with the elected representatives of the 'beleaguered minority' in the north.[84] What may, however, have finally swayed the Coalition government was the SDLP's emphasis on the vulnerability of its electoral support in any regime which lacked guarantees that the British state would be seriously prepared to reconsider its predominantly militarist approach to dealing with the Provisionals.

The problems that this created for the party can be illustrated from just one of what were regular occurrences. At the end of July, a major army and police operation sealed off many Catholic districts in Belfast and all cars and pedestrians entering and leaving were searched. The local party representative was forced to issue a florid denunciation of Whitelaw as a modern Cromwell.[85] It was precisely because the NIO was attempting, without any serious changes in security and internment policies, to integrate the SDLP that its intransigence on the Council of Ireland became the focus of negotiations.

The NIO calculated that the SDLP would in the end compromise and accept a predominantly internal settlement, because it needed something to justify its claims to compete with the Provisionals.[86] It was believed that the party was split between Belfast urban 'realists' and the 'country element', who, together with Hume from Derry, were seen as the more unreconstructed nationalists. There was some evidence that there was indeed a powerful faction in the party which was above all interested in getting into office.[87] However, British attempts to exploit these divisions and the NIO's rather banal machinations, were singularly unsuccessful in persuading the party to take a more realistic line on the disputed issues, particularly that of the Council of Ireland. But precisely because the concessions which the NIO had to offer on security and internment were patently cosmetic, it was eventually forced to make as if to yield some ground on the issue of the 'Irish Dimension.' It became increasingly clear that the NIO and SDLP positions on issues like internment and policing could not be reconciled. Their conflict instead was displaced onto another terrain, that of the 'Irish Dimension'. This shift is evident in two NIO papers prepared for the parties involved in the discussions on power-sharing.[88] Of the three major issues of internment, policing and a Council of Ireland, it was only on the last that significant progress was made. On internment, the basic policy of relating action to improvements in the security situation was unchanged, although this was sweetened by a promise in the second paper of a selective release of some internees before Christmas.[89] On policing, the problem of 'public support for and identification with the RUC' was recognised but actual proposals were minimalist.[90] To make these proposals more palatable, the possibility of an (undefined) role for a Council of Ireland in the area of 'law and order' was acknowledged. It was over the issue of a Council of Ireland that the most significant differences between the two documents became apparent. Thus, apart from its possible role in policing, the Council, which the first paper had said would have 'some executive functions and a consultative role', was now to have 'executive and harmonisation' functions. The notion of the harmonisation role of the Council of Ireland, was central to the SDLP's view of it as an institution with an active role in preparing the conditions for ultimate unity.

The Economist's comment on the interim agreement to form a power-sharing Executive was apt: 'It is a fragile package, for it is the product more of political ingenuity than of overwhelming public pressure and it may raise expectations, ... which cannot be fulfilled.'[91] The exact nature and powers of the Council of Ireland were left undefined. The later Sunningdale conference, between the British and Irish governments, and the parties involved in the Executive, was to settle this question. However, even then it proved impossible to resolve and the Executive entered office with this key issue given over to senior civil servants in Belfast and Dublin. The NIO may have believed that a greater familiarity with the major administrative problems of putting into effect grandiose notions about harmonisation would lead the SDLP leadership to scale down its ambitions. There is some evidence that this was occurring.[92] However the task of 'educating' the SDLP ministers was to prove very costly in political terms and was in fact fatal for the NIO's whole strategy.

The Protestant Response

The first significant manifestations of the 'Protestant backlash', as it was termed, came in the emergence of local vigilante groups in areas like north and west Belfast where, since August 1969, there had been frequent violent confrontations between Protestants and Catholics. The UDA had eventually emerged in September 1971 through a fusion of these groups in the period of intense post-internment violence.[93] Their response to the intensifying crisis of the state was to accuse the leading Unionist groups of adopting a policy of 'appeasement'. An early example of this type of reaction was a leaflet put out in 1970 in one of the first attempts in this period to mobilise Protestants at their places of work. It called on all 'loyalists' to write to their MPs demanding either the 'full restoration of law and order' or their resignations and it continued, 'Appeasement is cowardice and on looking back over the past few months we ask "what about the republican mobs from the Bogside" and compare this treatment to the use of CS gas by the Army in Belfast on loyalists . . . .'[94] (Reference to Protestant riots against Hunt Report). The Provisionals' adoption of an intense campaign of bombings in the spring of 1971 stimulated ideologies of embattlement, and the main Unionist daily speculated that such a threat would reproduce the classical Unionist pan-class unity of the Home Rule period and the IRA's 1918-21 offensive: 'They (the Provos) have brought together with one mind and one purpose all sections of pro-government opinion, from the humble labourer to the clergyman in his pulpit, from shipyard technician to surgeon in a hospital.'[95] Such attempts to conjure up the unities of the past fundamentally misconceived the nature of the current (unfolding) crisis. The one lesson which the British government and opposition were clearly learning was the impossibility of even managing the situation if any attempt was made to go back on the reforms of the state apparatuses initiated in 1969. Unionist unity was a chimera given the realisation of at least some sections of the leadership of the Unionist party that this 'reform' was irrevocable.

Nevertheless, the intensification of the Provisional campaign and the concomitant strengthening of the reactionary element in Unionist politics at all levels, did enable Brian Faulkner to persuade Heath's government that a radical anti-Provo measure was necessary if 'moderate' Unionism was to be preserved at all.

Inasmuch as internment failed to undermine the Provos, it also sealed the fate of Protestant moderation and represented its last attempt to preserve the Stormont regime.

During the months after the introduction of internment, Protestants were less and less united in their response to the military threat of the Provisionals. In September and October, William Craig, the dominant Unionist 'anti-appeaser', was only the most prominent of a group of Protestant politicians who addressed a series of large rallies (often composed of workers on their lunch hours), the main theme of which was to demand the creation of a 'third force'. This was in effect to demand that the British government sanction the recreation of the Protestant militia, the B Specials. Craig was the most hysterical of the Protestant politicians, claiming in one mass rally near the shipyards and aircraft factory that there were '1,500 armed terrorists backed by 3,000 auxiliaries in the Falls Road alone.'[96] John Taylor, a junior minister of Home Affairs, publicly supported these demands.[97]

Craig took these demands to the annual conference of the Unionist party in October. He opposed any further reforms, demanded full Stormont control over security, and proposed a resolution that was strongly critical of government security policies. This was defeated after a significant speech from Faulkner, who set out clearly the limits that the need to maintain British government support placed on them.

> Let us face realities. Legislative argument about Northern Ireland's constitutional responsibility for law and order is truly beside the point. Either we follow common security policies or we go it alone . . . our aim is not just to defeat the IRA. This is the first necessity but beyond it we must look to an Ulster united on a basis of common purpose rather than existing in a state of armed truce.[98]

But as the year drew to its close it became clearer that not only had Faulkner been correct to argue that Westminster would inevitably refuse to consider Craig's demands, but also that his own aim of being able to maintain a Unionist regime in power was unlikely to be realised. Already in November he was forced to react to speculation about a new and radical initiative.[99] As the year ended the press began to carry stories describing how the

Army was at last beginning to deal with the Provos. This was of little comfort to Faulkner, however, as it was also reported that the Army was one of the main forces pressing the government for a political initiative to complement[100] — as the Bloody Sunday killings were to show — the illusory nature of all talk of military progress.

Once direct rule became a real possibility, it became clear that Protestant politicians were far from agreed as to how to respond. Paisley, who had participated in rallies demanding a 'third force', at once differentiated his position from the rest by arguing for full integration in the event of the abolition of Stormont. Craig's Vanguard movement — with its mass rallies, strikes and its association with the UDA — was an expression of Ulster nationalism which treated direct rule as one symptom of the degeneration of Britain's traditional ruling class. In a pamphlet produced soon after direct rule, an *Economist* article which had claimed that most government ministers favoured a united Ireland as the ultimate solution, was quoted as one indication of the rot which had set in, 'The leftward shift in Westminster politics had produced a Conservative party tired, even bored with Irish politics from which they wish to extricate themselves.'[101] But, althoughVanguard had a significant amount of support from Protestant paramilitary groups, this was more a reflection of their sympathy for Craig's intransigent record as an opponent of republicanism and as a security hardliner, than an indentification with the specific policy of breaking the link with Britain in order to preserve some vague notion of Ulster 'nationhood'. Vanguard's talk of 'betrayal' had a clear resonance amongst the masses — to quote one early UDA paper.

> You, the Loyalist population have been sold to the terrorist. We were once a proud and happy nation, who sacrificed many of our best on far-away battlefields. They died in defence of a country that has now betrayed us. Ulster, another Palestine, another Suez, another Cyprus, another Aden. Our friends let us down, they broke under pressure.[102]

However, in practice, there was no natural tendency for such feelings of betrayal to develop into demands for UDI,[103] for the UDA was still very much a set of local organisations which lacked any clear strategy. Indeed, even after direct rule, they were primarily concerned to put pressure on the new administration to act against the 'No-Go' areas. Such demands, although they were embarrassing for Whitelaw, demonstrated that the paramilitaries still defined their function as one of putting pressure on the adminstration to act in particular ways rather than one of attempting radically to resist the new constitutional framework.[104]

It had been the clear evidence of divisions amongst Protestant political organisations, and the localistic and politically primitive nature of Protestant paramilitarism, which had persuaded the Heath administration that any Protestant reaction to direct rule would be relatively easy to contain.[105] These divisions and the incoherence of the Protestant working class response allowed the Whitelaw regime to under-estimate the problems they were facing, and to treat the question of Catholic disaffection as the primary consideration. It also appears to have encouraged a tendency amongst the SDLP and southern politicians to urge the Heath administration to press on with even more radical constitutional initiatives, irrespective of Protestant opposition.

The Sunningdale agreement was to prove disastrous for Faulkner's position inside the Unionist party. In November a resolution opposing power-sharing was only narrowly defeated at the Ulster Unionist Council, which was the party's main forum for debate on policy.[106] Faulkner had been effectively isolated at Sunningdale, as Heath and his officials joined with the SDLP and the southern government in pressing for an agreement which would satisfy the nationalists. The British view was typically cynical. Thus, the section of the communiqué concerned with the Council of Ireland was a pretty meaningless concession to nationalist sentiment, which in no way altered the substance of existing constitutional relations between Belfast and London.[107] Just as Whitelaw and the NIO expected the SDLP to welcome the opportunity to hold office, despite the effects of the continuation of internment and military activity on their supporters, so Faulkner was expected to be able to maintain his position in Protestant politics despite the insistence of prominent members of the SDLP that Sunningdale was a major victory for their conception of a Council of Ireland.[108]

In fact Sunningdale was to be the issue which allowed the hitherto divided Protestant opponents of direct rule and reform to establish a substantial degree of unity. A United Ulster Unionist Council had been founded in December, linking those Unionists who opposed power-sharing with Craig's Vanguard Unionist Party and Paisley's DUP.[109] The UUUC was to be massively successful in exploiting the many ambiguities of the Sunningdale communiqué, and particularly those concerning the role and powers of the Council of Ireland. Over five months after the agreement had been signed, in the middle of the Ulster Workers' Council strike, the new Labour Secretary of State, Merlyn Rees, would still be urging the executive to come to some agreement on the Council of Ireland.[110] At the same meeting, pathetically enough, it was recorded that 'support for the strike was based on a false understanding of Sunningdale. Once this had been removed by a clear agreed statement from the Executive support for the strikers would diminish.'[111] However, as even a sympathetic commentator was able to point out, the actions of the executive had contributed powerfully to such 'misapprehensions' amongst the masses — 'Instead of showing themselves to be a vigorous and reforming government, they spent the first months of their administration in continuous manoeuvring and debate on the implementation of the Sunningdale package.'[112] But it was precisely because the NIO had never had any intention of giving the new regime the power to implement 'vigorous' policies, that the largely clandestine horse-trading went on for five whole months. The SDLP's grandiose plans for a reconstruction of the RUC were ignored and internment was not revoked. Earlier proposals to deal with the low level of Catholic representation in the higher echelons of the civil service were likewise ignored. The executive's vacuous programme, 'Steps towards a Better Tomorrow', had been largely drawn up by the SDLP,[113] and would have little impact on the effective continuity in economic policy maintained by the conservative Department of Finance.[114] Faced with the reality of the British state's refusal to allow the executive any influence on the main lines of policy, the SDLP was faced with the choice of becoming a mere instrument of support for British strategy — clearly with potentially catastrophic effects on its support — or of trying desperately to get substantial concessions on the Council of Ireland.

It was the emasculation of the Executive which helps explain why, even after the disastrous effects of the British February general elections, the party continued, to the amazement of much 'informed' British comment, and the horror of the Unionists in the executive, to insist that there could be no 'watering down' of the Sunningdale agreement.[115] The UUUC won eleven of the twelve Northern Ireland seats at Westminster and the shaky and increasingly threadbare legitimacy of the Executive in the Protestant community was effectively destroyed. But the SDLP's own precarious position and the increasing internal stresses to which participation in the Executive was giving rise, meant that up to a few weeks before the outbreak of the strike its leadership was desperately hoping for the implementation of the Sunningdale agreement. The Executive members of the party seem to have had a touching Fabian faith in the neutrality of the bureaucracy in the period after direct rule. Thus, after a meeting between the Executive and the Coalition government at Hillsborough, at the beginning of February, it had been agreed to set up various working groups of northern and southern civil servants to investigate exactly what 'executive functions' the Council of Ireland could have. Their report, which was produced at the end of the month, clearly demonstrated that once the 'safe' areas like tourism, conservation and 'aspects of animal health' were agreed upon there was a basic incompatibility between the positions of the northern and southern groups. This was starkly set out in a report to Faulkner by the three NICS officials who had been in charge of the northern working groups. We will refer only to the most crucial, and in the light of subsequent events, telling difference. The southern proposal was that the Council should have full responsibility for electricity generation and distribution throughout Ireland. The three officials with obvious exasperation commented:

> It is to be doubted if much further explanation is needed as to why "all aspects of electricity generation and distribution" are unsuitable for executive action — this would involve giving the council sole responsibility under law . . . The Chairman of the NI Electricity Service has pointed out that possible adverse staff reac-

tions . . .could cause serious disruption. It has also been suggested that the public in the North who are opposed to a Council might take the excuse to withdraw payment of bills.[116]

The lack of enthusiasm of the Stormont bureaucracy for the whole project reflected the degree to which it was aware, as were the Unionist politicians, of the possible effects of some of the more grandiose SDLP notions on the Protestant masses. By this time the regime was so internally divided that the report was not made available to the whole Executive until almost two months after Faulkner had received it. At this point, the SDLP was thoroughly divided and demoralised: a substantial section of the Assembly party and the rank and file still pressed for a strong Council of Ireland whilst some of its executive members had been persuaded to go along with Faulkner in his plan for a 'phased introduction'.[117]

The whole power-sharing structure had become untenable. When the UWC strike began on 14 May, there were immediate demands from the SDLP and the southern government that Wilson and Rees use troops if necessary to maintain electricity supplies and defeat intimidation. Although Rees and Wilson periodically reassured the Executive of their total support, the army command in the north had no intention of using troops against the strikers to defend a regime which they were convinced would collapse anyway because of its acute internal divisions. A general who was in Northern Ireland at the time has subsequently revealed that in the Army's opinion the Executive was 'doomed before the strike ever began'. He went on to comment on the ironic compatibility between Rees's characteristics and the crisis: 'I think it was a mercy that Merlyn Rees was there at the time. He didn't make any decisions of any kind. If you'd had a decisive man who had arrested the strikers on the first day it would have created chaos and brought the province to the point of no return.'[118] The higher ranks of the NIO shared the army's view of the situation and thus Wilson was unlikely to risk a massive confrontation with the Protestants for the sake of an incapacitated Executive.[119] The UWC's success was dependent on the support of small groups of crucially situated power station workers, and on the intimidatory tactics of the UDA in the strike's earliest stages. Nevertheless, the claim by Rees and Executive members, particularly in the SDLP, that the strike was lacking in popular support was clearly spurious. Months of immobility produced by the Council of Ireland issue, coupled with open unwillingness of important sections of the SDLP to accept any dilution of their original proposals contributed to massive Protestant disaffection. It was only these general political and ideological conditions which allowed the power workers to consider embarking upon actions which might well have had horrendous results. In 1977, when conditions were substantially different, the second major attempt at a loyalist strike proved to be unable to mobilise these workers.[120]

The spectacular success of the strike led even informed commentators to exaggerate its strategic significance. Thus Fisk, who was to produce a serious and detailed narrative of the strike, claimed that it resulted in a breaking of the British will to stay in the north. Such a thesis greatly exaggerated the importance, in the period after direct rule had been introduced, attached to the establishment of a new governmental regime in the north. As our analysis of the White Paper has suggested, it implicitly assigned a merely supportive role to local politicians. A successful power-sharing arrangement would have been a useful adjunct to the new structures of 'permanent government' but it was in no sense essential. Failure to make this elementary but crucial distinction would continue to befuddle informed comments on British strategy over the next decade.

NOTES

1. Farrell, p. 287.
2. *Financial Times*, 16 November 1971.
3. *Observer*, 15 August 1971.
4. *Spectator*, 'Final Irish Solution' 18 December 1971.
5. House of Commons *Debates* vol 827, 29 November 1971, col 1586.
6. On Paisleyism in this period, see Smyth pp. 30-1 and Nelson pp. 102-3
7. House of Commons *Debates* vol 827, 25 November 1971, col 1587.
8. *Financial Times*, 26 November 1971.
9. Ibid, November 16 1971.
10. *Economist*, 12 January 1972.
11. Norton quotes Heath 'We were returned to office to change the course and the history of this nation.' p. 223.
12. Ibid, p. 226 and J Leruez, *Economic Planning and Politics in Britain* (London 1975) p. 238.

13. Joe Haines who was with Wilson when he met the SDLP in Belfast in November 1971 was typical: 'they spoke with more voices than there were members of the delegation. The greatest progress made was in the emptying of the Irish Whisky bottle.' (sic) *Politics of Power* (London 1977) p. 127.

14. *New Society*, 10 June 1971.

15. See Lord Windlesham, 'Ministers in Ulster: The Machinery of Direct Rule,' *Public Administration* 1973.

16. Bew *et al* chapters 2 and 3.

17. Thus Donnison reported a survey of 477 civil servants between the grades of Assistant Principal and Deputy Secretary where only 5% were Catholics — over 1/3 of NI's population are Catholics: *New Society* 5 7 73. In the higher reaches of 'sensitive' departments they were totally excluded eg. the Cabinet Office and Ministry of Home Affairs.

18. D Birrell and A Murie, *Policy and Government in Northern Ireland: Lessons of Devolution* (Dublin 1980) p. 141.

19. The NIO absorbed the crucial Home Affairs ministry from the start.

20. Thus the existing Stormont cabinet secretariat became a large component of the new Central Secretariat of the NIO but its members were acceptable either because they were thought of above average ability or because they were a useful source of information on their former masters. See D. Norman 'NIO Official Structure and Personnel' *Unpublished Paper*, Ulster Polytechnic 1982 and interview with former NIO junior minister.

21. P N Bell, 'The Northern Ireland Office in Comparative Context' paper given to panel on Territorial ministries in United Kingdom Central Government *Political Studies Assocation* Conference April 1982

22. *Northern Ireland Constitutional Proposals* (London HMSO 1973) p. 9.

23. David Watt commented 'The essence of the White Paper is that it asserts the sovereignty of Westminster over Northern Ireland more firmly than at any time since Ireland was divided.' *Financial times* 23 March 1973.

24. House of Commons *Debates* vol 837, 24 March 1972, col 241.

25. MacStiofain, p. 243 and *Republican News* 14 May 1972.

26. One of the most devastating explosions in Belfast's Lower Donegal Street killed two policemen and decimated the crew of a refuse lorry. *Belfast Newsletter* 21 March 1972.

27. *Financial Times* 4 April 1972.

28. See Robert Fisk article in The *Times* 23 June 1972.

29. John Whale 'How the IRA blew up its own cause' *Sunday Times* 11 March 1973.

30. *Republican News* 11 September 1971.

31. Rory O'Brady, president of Sinn Fein claimed that after a declaration of intent 'the element of reality would enter the situation at last . . . The fact is that the Unionist people of the North are very realistic and hard-headed and are not given to fighting lost causes. Keith Kyle,' The Provisionals' Regional Plan for a United Ireland' *The Listener* 16 March 1972.

32. *Times* 2 April 1972.

33. Provisionals opened fire on workers leaving Mackies engineering factory — a plant with a totally Protestant work force. *Times* 18 May 1972.

34. *Republican News* April 1971.

35. Ibid, 2 January 1972.

36. *Financial Times* 14 March 1972 and House of Commons *Debates* vol 833, 24 March 1972, col 1865.

37. By early June he had released nearly half — 470. *Times* 7 June 1972.

70

38. *Times* 27 May 1972.

39. Ibid, 2 and 6 June 1972.

40. Ibid, 14 June 1972.

41. *Sunday Times* 11 March 1973.

42. The two officials were Philip Woodfield and Frank Steele. Woodfield was the most senior member of NIO with a knowledge of the North — he had been the head of the Northern Ireland Department in the Home Office in the two years before direct rule. Steele on secondment from the Foreign Office was head of the NIO 'Political Affairs' section. It was perhaps symptomatic that Woodfield, who was to return to Northern Ireland in 1980 as head of NIO was an expert on prison reform. The *Times* 'Diary — living with Northern Ireland crisis for two years' 1 July 1972.

43. *Times* 16 June 1972.

44. Ibid, 23 June 1972.

45. *Times* 28 June 1972.

46. They demanded a response on three demands — the British government to recognise the right of the whole of the people of Ireland to decide its future; a declaration of intent to withdraw on or before 1 January 1973; a general amnesty for all 'political prisoners' in Irish and British jails. The *Times* 11 July 1972.

47. See David Wood, 'Losing Friends and Influencing Enemies' The *Times* 17 July 1972.

48. Seamus Twomey, IRA commander in Belfast called a press conference in Andersonstown in which he claimed that a restored truce was possible. The *Times* 13 July 1972.

49. *Financial Times* 15 July 1972. Joe Haines reported of the meeting between Wilson himself and O'Connell and Joe Cahill 'Though he and his colleagues were to us light years away from reality, especially when discussing what was politically possible, he demonstrated an intellectual quality greater than many politicians we had met in Northern Ireland. He is a man not to be underestimated.' Haines p. 126.

50. The rather sensational account of the young middle class Dubliner who had an affair with O'Connell at this time claims that O'Connell 'was a little seduced by the notion of political power.' Maria McGuire, *To Take Arms* (London 1973) p. 120

51. See *Fortnight* 7 September 1972. It claimed there was a split between 'those still looking for a solution through violence and those who want to redirect along more traditional lines.'

52. On republican ideology see Bob Purdie, 'Reconsiderations of Republicanism and Socialism' in A Morgan and B Purdie eds. *Ireland Divided Nation Divided Class* (London 1980).

53. *Times* 19 and 21 July 1972.

54. Ibid, 28 July 1972.

55. House of Commons *Debates* vol 823, 22 September 1971, col 26.

56. See Downey, p.64-65.

57. Even before direct rule the Irish Cabinet had met to consider more stringent controls on republicans in the Republic — *Financial Times* 4 January 1972.

58. *Fortnight* 2 August 1972.

59. McAlister, p. 120.

60. *Fortnight* 7 September 1972. Dennis Kennedy reported on Dublin government attitudes: 'Despite the fulsome communiqués of agreement all round there is increasing disillusion with the former heroes of the North. Dublin policy — Government and non-Government — has long been based on the hope that the

SDLP would provide the rigorous political leadership that would keep Catholic opinion in the North out of the hands of the IRA. But this does not mean, whatever the ambiguity of its own position, that the government wants the SDLP to do this by reverting to a revised Nationalist Party calling for a United Ireland or nothing. The SDLP is arguably "greener" now than any party in Dublin.' *Fortnight* 5 October 1972.

61. *Irish Times* 31 October 1972. The degree to which even usually realistic constitutional Nationalists were capable of putting grandiose interpretations forward was clear in an article by the UCD historian Ronan Fanning: 'The phrase, the Irish Dimension, may well prove among the documents' most enduring contributions to the present Anglo-Irish debate. . . . Ulster Protestants might well conclude that the phrase was intended as a less emotive and hopefully less provocative synonym for the demands made by Mr Lynch and the SDLP for a British declaration in favour of eventual Irish Unity.' *Spectator* 4 November 1972.

62. *The Future of Northern Ireland: A Paper for Discussion* (London HMSO 1972) p. 33.

63. House of Commons *Debates* vol 846, 13 November 1972, cols 45-48.

64. Ibid, col 109.

65. Farrell p. 301.

66. Official figures clearly demonstrate the extent of 'terrorist' activity. In 1969 there were 8 explosions, no shootings and 13 deaths. In 1972 there were 1,495 explosions, 10,628 shootings and 467 deaths. K Boyle, T Hadden and P Hillyard *Ten Years On In Northern Ireland* (London 1980) p. 15.

67. At the end of the year Robert Fisk could report that the Provos were 'badly mauled, in parts of Belfast beaten into virtual extinction.' *Times* 1 December 1972. However within a couple of months there was a major series of gunbattles with the army resulting in ten deaths over one weekend. *Times* 5 February 1973. The problems which their military activities created for the Provisionals in terms of potential popular war-weariness and resentment were clearly revealed. In a prolonged gun battle in the New Lodge area three Provisionals and three civilians were killed. *Republican News* reported '40,000 mourn murdered victims of British massacre' 9 February 1973. But as Burton notes in his important study of the relationship between Provisionals and the local population in the most beleaguered of Catholic ghettos — Ardoyne — there was considerable resentment at Provo confrontations which threatened massive army retribution. Frank Burton, *The Politics of Legitimacy: Struggles in a Belfast Community* (London 1978) p. 82-94.

68. *Unfree Citizen* 13 November 1972.

69. See for example the PD's attack on the SDLP. 'They are out to channel the discontent of the Northern minority away from the dangerous revolutionaries and back into the parliamentary system.' *Unfree Citizen* 21 August 1972.

70. Its position here was somewhat eased by the Provisionals' own agreement to a truce and negotiations while internment continued.

71. McAlister, pp 122-3 and Paul Arthur, 'Independence' in D Rea (ed) *Political Co-Operation in Divided Societies* (Dublin 1982) p. 124.

72. Austin Currie *Irish News* 3 October 1973.

73. Thus the *Irish News* on the possibility of direct rule — 'Direct rule would be a legitimate step towards reunification which must come.' 2 February 1972.

74. See eg. *Republican News* 2 June 1973 and *Unfree Citizen* 21 August 1972.

75. Paddy Devlin of the SDLP told a union conference 'if the SDLP were returned to the Assembly with 25% of seats the entire face of Northern Ireland politics would change.' *Republican News* 23 June 1973.

76. Michael Laver, *The Theory and Practice of Party Competition: Ulster* 1973-75 (London and Beverly Hills 1976) p. 34.

77. Ibid.

78. Michael Gallagher, *The Irish Labour Party in Transition 1957-82* (Manchester and Dublin 1982) pp. 203-210.

79. *Irish News* 3 July 1973.

80. Northern Ireland Constitutional Proposals pp. 29-30.

81. At the first meeting of SDLP representatives who had been elected to the Assembly 'It was agreed that a delegation . . . would see the Taoiseach on the present government's statements on the National Unity issue which indicates a clear drift away from the stance of the last government. It was thought by the group that assurances on the issues being negotiated between ourselves and the British government would greatly strengthen our hand. Equivocation similar to that emanating from Coalition government spokesmen could be damaging to us at a time when we appear to be on the verge of a breakthrough.' Minutes of meeting of Assembly Party held in Dungannon 6 July 1973.

82. Minutes of SDLP Assembly Party 19 September 1973

83. Minutes of SDLP Assembly Party meeting 19 September 1973.

84. One former member of the party who was involved in these negotiations referred to 'an element of implicit blackmail' in relations with southern governments. Interview with Paddy Devlin.

85. *Irish News* 30 July 1973.

86. *Economist* 27 Ocotber 1973.

87. These terms were used by a senior British civil servant who was at this time in the NIO in an interview with one of the authors.

88. The first NIO paper *Inter-Party Discussions* is dated 19 November 1973, the latter is undated but is clearly the one which sums up positions at the time of agreement to form an executive.

89. The second paper dropped a risible paragraph included in the earlier paper. This had dealt with the conditions under which the Secretary of State might exercise his powers of selective release and revealed graphically the NIO's lack of awareness of conditions in the main Catholic ghettos. It included 'advice on behaviour in custody, the availability of stable home conditions and regular employment . . . .'

90. On the crucial area of complaints and their handling the NIO proposals were vague and non-committal. *Law and Order and Policing* (nd).

91. *Economist* 24 November 1973.

92. One example comes from the case of the SDLP minister Paddy Devlin whose responsibility was Health and Social Services. In January 1974 the permanent secretary to the Office of the Executive had asked departments for their assessment of prospects for involvement of the Council of Ireland in their field of responsibility. Devlin's permanent secretary replied in a way that — other interviews have tended to imply — was the general bureaucratic response in both Belfast and Dublin: 'You will see that we have nothing of moment to suggest at this stage, and only vague contingencies in mind for the future. Generally our view is that the onus lies on the Republic to bring its services up to the standards prevailing in Northern Ireland before there could be any real scope for joint schemes . . . .' N Dugdale to K P Bloomfield 24 January 1974.

93. Nelson, p. 105.

94. Leaflet produced by *Ulster Committee for the Defence of the Constitution 1970*.

95. *Belfast Newsletter* 2 September 1971.

96. *Belfast Newsletter* 7 September 1971.

97. Ibid, 14 September 1971.

98. *Belfast Newsletter* 14 October 1971.

99. Ibid 6 November 1971.

100. See article by Peter Jenkins *Guardian* 17 January 1972.

101. *Ulster, a Nation* (Belfast, April 1972).

102. *The Attack* (Bulletin No. 2 March 1972).

103. Nelson comments perceptively on the predominantly bourgeois cadre of Vanguard and its reactionary social and economic philosophy, pp. 109-112.

104. The Englishman who played a leading role in the UDA in this period and later sold his story to the *Sunday Times* gives a graphic description of the political primitiveness of the organisation. Thus of an early meeting between the UDA's Army Council and Whitelaw: 'There we were with the top man and everyone started contradicting each other. They talked about their individual areas rather than general issues. Very naive. It probably helped Whitelaw.' 'Big Dave lifts the Mask.' *Sunday Times* 28 January 1973.

105. *Observer* 26 March 1972.

106. Farrell, p. 310.

107. A senior NIO official at the time described the Council of Ireland as 'a sham' in the sense that the fact that the Council of Ministers had to work on the basis of a unanimity rule meant there was no danger to the Unionist position. Interview with one of the authors.

108. See Mervyn Pauley's article on this point, *Belfast Newsletter* 1 June 1974.

109. Nelson, ibid., p. 139.

110. Minutes of Executive meeting 20 May 1974 EXMIN 74/72.

111. Ibid.

112. *Fortnight* 7 June 1974.

113. An SDLP internal document had noted in particular 'the complete absence of Catholics in senior posts in certain strategic sections — particularly Stormont Castle and the Ministry of Finance' and recommended a 'few strategic appointments' of Catholics. On the programme see McAlister, p. 133.

114. Thus one of the first things the Executive considered was a report on economic and physical planning drawn up by the Ministry of Finance. Its purpose was to explain how that section of the White Paper on 'reconstruction and development' was to be implemented. Its tone was panglossian and minimalist with a predictable penchant for blaming 'instability' for the north's profound economic problems. 'Social, Economic and Physical Planning' Report to the Northern Ireland Executive *Department of Finance* (January 1974) p. 3.

115. See *Economist* 13 April 'the Council of Ireland is a dead duck until the security forces get on top of terrorism.'

116. All quotes from Report of three officials who included the head of NICS and secretary to Executive *EX Memo 77/74* 1 May 1974. Other differences of a substantial nature occurred on its possible functioning in 'Culture and Arts' — 'For a government to hand over its functions in respect of arts and culture to some international authority would be to abdicate its basic responsibility', and on the funding of the Council.

117. See R Fisk, *The Point of No Return: The Strike which Broke the British in Ulster* (London 1975) p. 159.

118. *Irish Times*, 15 May 1984.

119. Interview with ex-member of the NIO who was in the north at this time.

120. Something of the 'doomsday' flavour of the period is evoked in a few extracts from a *Situation Report* prepared for the Executive on 20 May — six days into the strike: 'Electricity: Very critical . . . .producing less than 30% normal

Monday load . . . . Increasing concern about continual lack of maintenance. The whole system may suddenly black out: there would then be no power for 3 — 4 days. Sewerage: could be critical in 48 hours if there is heavy rain. Danger of pollution.'

3

The Contradictions of Ulsterisation
1974-1979

The success of the UWC strike provoked both outrage and fatuous optimism inside the Labour Party. Thus, while Renée Short demanded that if the UWC called another strike the government should 'go in with tanks',[1] in Northern Ireland, Rees and his deputy Stanley Orme, who had consistently refused to meet the UWC during the strike, and had denounced them as crypto-fascists, now began to talk of the radical potentialities of the new 'working-class consciousness' allegedly embodied in the strike. A new popular nationalism was detected. In the Commons emergency debate Rees attributed the cause of the strike not to any policy decisions made in Belfast, Dublin or London, but to the emergence of a new ideological phenomenon: ' . . . . a new form of Protestant nationalism had been emerging in Ulster, culminating in the events of the past few weeks.'[2] The White Paper setting out a plan for the election of a Constitutional Convention, which was supposedly to draft an agreed plan for the future government of Northern Ireland, took up what was to be an important, if never satisfactorily defined theme of policy for the next two years:

> It has become clear during recent discussions in Northern Ireland
> that many people will welcome an opportunity of this kind. This
> belief has been strengthened by a new awareness in the Protestant
> and Catholic working class of their real interests and by their wish
> to play a real part in political activity . . . in recent months various
> groups within the community have shown an increased desire to
> participate in the political process and a growing belief that they
> can best find for themselves political relationships which will be

> acceptable to them. The government believes it is essential that participation in these processes should take place not only between like-minded groups but equally between groups which hold apparently strongly opposed views . . . [3]

This notion of a newly acquired working-class consciousness was certainly ill-defined. Did it mean the UWC which Rees and Orme had so recently bitterly denounced? Did it include the recently legalised UVF and Sinn Fein? Such a notion was also at odds with the section of the White Paper which set out a 'number of facts to be recognised', namely, that there had to be some form of power-sharing or partnership; that any proposals had to be acceptable to 'the people of the United Kingdom as a whole', and that 'Northern Ireland unlike the rest of the United Kingdom shares a common land frontier and a special relationship with another country, the Republic of Ireland. Any political arrangement must recognise and provide for this special relationship. There is an Irish Dimension.'[4]

A *Times* leader correctly caught the flavour of the situation: '. . . the events of the past three weeks have left the curators of policy at Westminster floundering. Most of them are willing to admit that the situation and possibilities in Northern Ireland have been radically altered by these events, while few of them are willing to admit that this requires any radical amendment of policy.'[5] If the substance of policy remained unchanged, the vague references to the working class did signify the re-opening of channels of communication with 'non-constitutional' organisations. Some commentators (and, it would seem, both Rees and Stanley Orme) were entranced with the radical potentialities of the post-strike situation.[6] However, the Constitutional Convention and the new contacts with the NIO's Political Affairs section, working out of Laneside,[7] were not, in fact, indications of some new strategy. Rather they were specifically designed to keep local political and military forces harmlessly occupied whilst consideration was given to the possibilities of some new departure in British policy.[8] Wilson was to make one last attempt at a constitutional initiative. A cabinet sub-committee chaired by him discussed a series of options from the end of the strike into 1975. Withdrawal was considered at a series of meetings over a period of three months. The other main possibilities discussed were repartition and the creation of a 'no-man's land' along the border with the Republic. The committee ended up rejecting all three possibilities, arguing that all of them would probably aggravate the problem still further.[9] Thus, by early 1975, the Labour government had ruled out any radical constitutional initiative. At the same time there was no inclination to attempt any other type of transformative policy in any area in the north.

Instead there was the complacent and self-serving assumption that the British state had done all it could to reform and improve conditions in the north and that the existing impasse was therefore attributable to the primitivism of local politicians. The exasperation which Callaghan had begun to express along these lines in 1970 was now much more intense and by 1977 one commentator could report that his current view was that 'the Irish will have to be left to sweat it out for a while if they are ever to come to their senses.'[10] Insofar as there was an impasse, it was in fact a direct product of the inherent limitations of the only two strategies which the British state had been capable of developing towards the north.

Its first strategy, which had involved various 'plans' to try and extricate itself from Northern Ireland, had failed because both constitutional and militarist nationalists had proved unable to subdue the Protestants.[11] The second strategy was to eliminate the most obviously discriminatory features of the state and to increase its effective subordination to the central government in London. However, this approach did nothing to alter the deeper causes of sectarian division, one of the most crucial of which was the economic inequality of Protestants and Catholics. It shared, with the first strategy, a strong disposition to minimize the costs of continuing involvement and, though clearly more realistically aware of the forces in play, its main objective was to manipulate and domesticate rather than to transform or to eradicate. The unintended and contradictory effects of this strategy would be clearly revealed in the long truce with the Provisionals which took place in 1975.

The Politics of the Truce

The autumn of 1974 saw an intensification of Provo activity in the north and on the mainland. It began with the assassination of two judges in Belfast[12] and continued with an English bombing campaign, culminating in the Birmingham bombs, which killed 21 people at the end of November. In the north there was a sharp increase in sectarian assassinations of Catholics.[13] In the Westminster elections of that month the overall UUUC vote rose from 51% to 58% of the poll.[14] The *Times* commented 'Ulster voters have retreated to their sectarian stockades at the polling booths as never before.'[15] It was soon morosely toying with the idea that the whole Convention strategy should be dropped, although it finally concluded that it was probably 'better now to go through the motions prescribed by the government in its White Paper . . . '[16]

Such views were commonplace especially after the election. It was therefore speculated that, as the government could not have expected much of positive effect to issue from the Convention, the real purpose had been to use the inevitably rancorous results as an excuse for disengagement. One commentator reported an atmosphere of 'decaying colonialism' at Stormont,

> . . . optimism about the success of British politics in Northern Ireland has become a rare quality among the English ministers and civil servants . . . The word 'withdrawal' may not yet be said in the corridors at more than a whimper but of the certitude which Powell seeks there is none. (In his election campaign Enoch Powell had emphasised the need for 'certitude' about the status of Northern Ireland in the United Kingdom.)[17]

An announcement of withdrawal had come to seem imminent and, in the course of the following year, there was intense speculation as to when it would take place. As late as 1978 two *Sunday Times* journalists were still claiming that such a policy was the real British strategy. The first clear evidence of this, they claimed, were the secret talks between senior members of the NIO and the Provos, which began in early 1975.[18] It was these negotiations which led to a relatively long-lived 'Truce' between the Provos and the Army and RUC in 1975.

The motivation on the British side was the increasing evidence that the UWC strike had caused the leadership of the Provisionals to feel more optimistic about the imminence of radical changes in British policy. At the centre of this optimism was a particular interpretation of the significance of the UWC strike. The Provisionals' own opposition to Sunningdale led them to see considerable potential in the actions of the loyalist workers: 'The loyalist workers are now capable of throwing up their own leaders and will not, in future, be led by the nose by middle-class, careerist politicians or the landed gentry of Ulster Unionism.'[19] This view was reinforced by the efforts of the UWC and loyalist paramilitaries to establish a political leadership divorced from the UUUC. Reports that a three-day conference of loyalist groups would agree to talks with the Provisionals were warmly welcomed by the latter:

> There is evidence that the working-class Protestants who comprise the paramilitary groups are strongly Socialist in their thinking. This bodes ill for traditional Unionist politicians . . . who have exploited the loyalist working class on the basis of sectarianism. This development could have far-reaching effects if they realise, as they must surely do in time, their community of interest with the depressed Catholic working class.[20]

Not everyone in the Provisional movement was as optimistic. The *Republican News* columnist 'Vindicator' attacked the notion that the recent moves by the loyalist paramilitaries indicated 'a significant change in the mentality of the Orange colonists who have for 180 years been the major agents in upholding English imperialism in Ireland.'[21] Despite 'Vindicator's' dire warnings of the dangers of pursuing the policy of détente[22] the Provisionals responded positively to the UDA's apparent change of direction. When Andy Tyrie offered to negotiate with the Provisionals, the Belfast Sinn Fein leader Marie Drumm declared 'we are at all times willing to sit at the conference table with the representatives of the UWC.'[23] As one after another the loyalist paramilitaries declared ceasefires during the summer and autumn of 1974, some Republicans became quite euphoric. One described the UWC strike as 'brilliantly conceived and executed . . . Britain does not need Ulster Loyalists but Ireland does.'[24]

The policy of détente continued, with internment providing an increasingly important common denominator between the Provisionals and the Loyalists. A twelfth of July message from the Provisionals was paraphrased by the *Irish News*: 'Internment must be ended and the voice of the working class demonstrated through Loyalist groups and the Republican movement.'[25] The British government encouraged discussions between the para-militaries, in and out of prison, and Stanley Orme admitted that he had been involved in round-table negotiations with Provisional, Official and Loyalist leaders in Long Kesh.[26]

Co-operation inside Long Kesh helped to sustain the Republican/Loyalist détente outside. The Provisional leadership appear to have been much more optimistic than the Loyalists: 'The old chasm between Unionists and Nationalists had been considerably narrowed . . . frequent communication and discussion is taking place between grassroots loyalists and Republicans.'[27] The Provisionals' optimism about the possibility of reaching an accommodation with 'grassroots' loyalism was necessarily complementary to their analysis of the strategy of the British state. The Provisional leadership had long since forsaken the notion that Britain had any desire to stay in Ireland. Indeed, belief that Britain wished to withdraw underpinned the Provisionals' analysis of the post-Executive period. In June, a leading Republican, Sean Keenan, confidently declared 'the fight is almost over. The British troops are ready to withdraw.'[28] The Convention was received as further evidence of British intentions. The Provisionals believed that London had no illusions about its inevitable failure, and that the decision to set it up was therefore intended to make British public opinion 'ripe' for the final step — a declaration of intent to withdraw.[29]

By August the Provisionals' analysis was fully formed. In a statement, worth quoting at length, the leadership declared:

> The deliberate inaction and vagueness of British government policy is designed to increase uncertainty among Loyalists and Unionists and to encourage them to take up entrenched positions. When the time comes for the Loyalist/Unionist elements to make agreed proposals to the British government the hard-line group's proposals will be unacceptable. The time will then be ripe for the British government to make its appeal to British public opinion

> . . . The Pilate-like washing of hands will be ceremoniously carried out and will be heartily endorsed by the mass of the British people . . . A dignified withdrawal is then possible with little loss of face and considerable financial benefit to the British taxpayer.[30]

There was increasing evidence of the desire of the Provisional leadership to discuss the situation with representatives of Protestant opinion. In the autumn and early winter of 1974 various contacts had been made and these culminated in a meeting in Feakle, Co Clare, between a group of Protestant clergy and six members of the PIRA Army Council. In their account of the meeting, two of the clergy claimed that in the discussion, 'It became clear that there were "hawks" and "doves" in the Army Council . . . Our strategy was to try and strengthen the "doves". There were clearly those who inclined to the view that it would at that juncture be right to call a cease–fire and "go political".'[31] The delegation left a series of proposals for the Provos to consider as a basis for a permanent ceasefire. In its reply the Army Council set out its demands. The IRA then declared a temporary ceasefire to enable the government to reply to their proposals. In the Commons Rees outlined the government's response: the Army had been able to reduce the size and frequency of patrols, it had also largely avoided the need to question people and search their homes. Significantly, Rees had not signed an interim custody order since the ceasefire began. The scaling down of activities would continue and if there was a permanent cessation of violence the Army could be reduced to a 'peace-time level.' He also promised that if there is a 'genuine and sustained end of violence, I shall progressively release detainees. Once I am satisfied that violence has come to a permanent end, I shall be prepared to speed up the rate of releases with a view to releasing all detainees.'[32] He also made it clear that his officials had been and were available to 'hear the views of those in Northern Ireland who have something to contribute to the solution of its problems.' Rees listed organisations with which discussions had already taken place — the UDA, UVF, the Volunteer Political Party and added that the same opportunities existed for Provisional and Official Sinn Fein.

In the middle of January it became known that Rees had

authorised talks between his officials and Sinn Fein.[33] Within a day of the announcement of an indefinite ceasefire, on 10 February, a Provisional source was outlining the main elements of the 12 points which they were to claim had been agreed in their negotiations with the British. As some of these were, to say the least, controversial, the NIO always denied that there had been any such agreement.[34]

In fact there was clear evidence that some, at least, of the twelve points were in operation. There was a sharp reduction in Army and RUC activity in Catholic areas.[35] Seven 'incident centres' were set up, each manned by Sinn Fein officials in constant touch with an operations room in Stormont Castle — manned by NIO and Ministry of Defence officials.[36] For both the Irish government and the SDLP the incident centres were seen as dangerous concessions which could only build up the Provos' political credibility.[37] The guarantee of immunity for certain leading Provos became an issue when the Ulster Unionist MP James Molyneux asked Rees in the Commons why Seamus Twomey was not arrested when he was spotted by soldiers in Belfast.[38] Robert Fisk, the most knowledgable of the British correspondents in Belfast at the time, claimed that photographs of Twomey had been removed from several battalions' operations rooms in Belfast. More importantly he went to the heart of the questions of the truce, namely, British acquiescence in an open and high profile for the Provos in Catholic areas, '. . .if these concessions were never made how was a Provisional able to control traffic on the Falls Road with impunity . . . while brazenly holding a machine pistol in his hand.'[39]

One of the Feakle clergymen, William Arlow, claimed that the Provisionals had been given an undertaking by the British officials that if the Convention collapsed the British would begin the process of withdrawal.[40] The Provisional leadership appears to have been convinced that this was exactly what their negotiations had achieved. David O'Connell claimed that 'The overall feature of that truce was a statement by the British government that it was committed to disengage from Ireland but it could not say so publicly.'[41] Since the negotiations were solely with the NIO officials at Laneside, this was more a sign of naiveté on O'Connell's part than of any secret British strategy. In fact,

Provisional convictions and the fears of other groups, from the UDA to the SDLP and the Cosgrave government, were a deliberate product of the operation of the NIO's political affairs section. Together with Frank Cooper, the permanent under secretary at Stormont Castle, they were prepared to discourse at length with the Provisionals on the question of withdrawal. Although it would be rationalised later as an attempt to educate the Provisionals into the complexities of the situation, it appears to have had a more substantial motivation. The *Irish Times* Northern correspondent at the time was subsequently to recall a dinner party given for local newspaper editors by Rees and Cooper at which Cooper had said that withdrawal would come in about five years. He added that in the first two months of 1975 'officials at Stormont began to lace their dinner conversations and political *tête á têtes* with predictions of a pull out. It now seems that this was aimed at creating an atmosphere which would convince the Provos that their main aim, a declaration of intent, was soon to become a reality.'[42]

The period of the ceasefire saw an actual increase in the level of violence. In the first nine months following the truce, 196 people were killed in political violence, 37 more than in the equivalent period in 1974.[43] Rees responded to this with the unconvincing claim that the ceasefire and the violence were quite distinct, and he laid the blame for the latter on 'interfactional feuding (the armed conflict between the Official IRA and the break away Irish Republican Socialist Party) and sectarian murders.'[44] However, as there was evidence of unofficial Provisional involvement in the feud and as a major precipitant of the sectarian violence was what Protestant paramilitaries saw as British endorsement of the increasingly prominent profile of the Provos in Catholic areas, the distinction was unconvincing. Rees's position was further undermined by evidence that the Provisionals' own commitment was becoming increasingly strained. In May, after the killing of an RUC man in Derry, he was reduced to explaining lamely that the NIO had been able to use the incident centres to establish that it had been the Provisionals who were responsible. This marked a curious reversal of their original role — to prevent violence.[45] Later in the year, after the IRA had killed four soldiers in South Armagh, Rees pathetically confided to the

Commons: 'I could not with my hand on my heart say that I do not speak with many people in Northern Ireland who are accomplices of a lot of funny people in Northern Ireland.'[46] In the autumn there was a series of bombings.[47] The *Times* correspondent noted, . . . 'officials are privately anxious that the so-called cease-fire should continue. Not only do they sincerely believe that it is saving lives and property, but they acknowledge that much of government policy is based on its longevity . . .'[48]

In November the government closed the incident centres but the Provos claimed that contacts with the government continued and that there was still a 'truce situation.' On 5 December Rees ordered the release of the last 75 detainees, 57 of whom were members of the Provisionals.[49]

The cease-fire ended on 23 January but contacts were maintained. In a recent analysis of Provisional strategy, a sympathetic observer sees this period as a watershed in the history of the organisation,

> The leadership then, and in particular David O'Connell believed that the British could be negotiated into a settlement or at least that the appearance of negotiations with the IRA would so destabilise the British positions in the eyes of the Northern Unionists, and indeed of the established politicians North and South of the border, that they would have no option but to disengage.[50]

The cease-fire was severely to divide the Provos. As one member put it: 'Suppose we get the release of all detainees, an amnesty and withdrawal of troops to barracks, we are still back where we started in 1969.'[51] It is in the nature of the Republican movement that policy disputes rarely take place in public. The cease-fire increased the frequency with which internal disagreement over politicial aims was revealed. This was first seen in February 1975, when it was announced that the IRA in Belfast was operating as a 'temporary police force' in Republican areas, acting under the control of the incident centres.[52] Belfast Sinn Fein repudiated the Dublin statement and blamed a breakdown in communications.[53] Subsequently IRIS, *An Phoblacht* and *Republican News* were dominated by a discussion of the issue.* In the

---

*We are grateful to Denis Norman for his unpublished analysis of Catholic politics in the period.

end the refusal of the Belfast Brigade of PIRA to perform any policing function effectively put an end to the debate.[54] Further divisions were revealed in the course of a debate over participation in the Convention elections.[55] Perhaps the most serious disagreement within the movement arose over internment. In March 1975, the Belfast Sinn Fein organiser denied repeated allegations that the truce had resulted in the abandonment of the demand for the immediate release of the internees.[56] Criticism of the leadership reached its height in August when the movement, in keeping with its prediction of imminent victory, replaced the traditional anti-internment demonstrations with an 'Anti-Internment Festival.' Although internment would be ended by Christmas many Republicans apparently felt that it was inappropriate to hold a festival while internment was still in operation.[57] Most disturbing for the leadership was the almost unprecedented appearance of letters from internees criticising the festival.[58]

Nevertheless, the Provisional leadership did largely retain the loyalty of the internees and sentenced prisoners. This was to be demonstrated when the NIO announced the ending of special category status. It was the loyalist prisoners and their supporters who led the opposition to the withdrawal of political status. The Provisional reaction to Rees's announcement — that it was a 'foolish' decision — once again demonstrated their belief that the eventual declaration to withdraw would resolve all secondary issues.[59] The loyalty of the Republican prisoners was not in question, but the effect of the leadership's strategy on their morale was reported to be serious.[60]

The leadership could not depend upon the same degree of loyalty from the rest of the movement. As early as Easter 1975 the Provisionals in Newry closed the town's incident centre and began a series of major attacks on the RUC and Army. Operating under the title of the South Armagh Republican Action Force, this faction turned increasingly to sectarian murder: five Protestants were murdered in the Tullyvallen Orange Hall in September 1975 and in January 1976 a works bus carrying Protestant workers was stopped in South Armagh, the Catholic driver separated from his passengers, who were then machine-gunned, and ten of whom were killed.[61] The Derry Provisionals were also noted for their opposition to the ceasefire and eventually closed their centre by blowing up the building in which it was housed.[62] Rumours that the Belfast rank-and-file were unhappy with the truce were to be confirmed during the 'Anti-Internment Festival.' Despite apparently genuine appeals from Sinn Fein leaders for a peaceful festival, the Belfast brigade used the demonstrations to precipitate the most bitter outbreak of street violence for years. The mood of the Belfast volunteers was evident from the determination of many of them to take on the British Army in open and armed confrontation.[63]

The threat of defection from the Provisionals' Belfast brigade was increased by the formation of the Irish National Liberation Army, the military wing of the IRSP, and by its adoption of an overtly offensive military strategy. In spite of Provisional efforts to suppress the INLA it was reported that many PIRA volunteers had already defected.[64] The leadership required some way in which the members could be involved in 'active service' other than the undirected attacks on the Army and RUC in which they were increasingly involved. It was principally for this reason that it sanctioned the pogrom of Official Republicans and the occasional blitz of commercial targets.[65]

Growing signs of divisions within the leadership were evidence that the efforts to secure the cease–fire against internal opposition had not been entirely successful. More than anything else the continued commitment to the incident centres came to symbolise the differences in the movement. At the Sinn Fein Ard Fheis, Rory O'Brady made his personal support for the centres clear when he described them as 'the very legs on which the truce stands.' Prominent Belfast Sinn Feiners like Marie Drumm were also identified as being fully behind the centres, on the grounds that they constituted a 'power-base for Sinn Fein.'[66] When the NIO withdrew from the centres on 11 November 1975, the supporters of the centres were inevitably embarrassed. O'Brady's request for a 'clarification' from the British indicated his own discomfiture.

As the British government continued to ease itself out of the cease–fire during the winter of 1975-76, some members of Sinn Fein continued to express support for the truce, in spite of the IRA's increasingly bloody actions in Northern Ireland and

Britain.[67] Perhaps the final blow to those in favour of a revived truce was Harold Wilson's declaration, on recalling the Convention, that a United Ireland was neither a practical proposition nor a solution which any party in Britain would wish to impose.[68] The symbolic end of the cease–fire came with the British Army's raid on the Falls' Road centre and the resignation of Sinn Fein's Belfast organiser.[69] With its morale badly affected, and with major divisions still unhealed,[70] a revised Provisional leadership attempted to restore both unity and morale in an all too familiar manner. In early 1976, in a shake-up of the Provisional hierarchy, Sean MacStiofain returned to the Army Council.

Labour politicians and members of the NIO have been quite prepared to admit that the purpose of the truce was to divide and weaken the Provisionals and to get rid of internment, as prelude to reasserting the rule of law and treating Provisional actions as criminal.[71] Rees's bumbling performance was quite appropriate to a period in which obfuscation was central to state policy.[72] The true nature of that policy would be fully revealed at Westminster in 1976, when Rees revealed that soon after the end of the truce and the release of the last detainees, a committee had been set up by the NIO to investigate the problem of 'securing greater effectiveness of the police in enforcing the rule of law.'[73] Although the Bourne Committee had been instructed to consider the question of police 'acceptability' it was mainly concerned to recommend an increase in the RUC's effectiveness.[74] With not a hint of embarrassment for the period of nearly a year when he had sanctioned the Provisionals' imposition of their own conceptions of order on large areas of Northern Ireland, Rees now defined the 'security problem' as one 'of small groups of criminals.'[75]

How can one explain the Provisionals' readiness to accept the illusions about withdrawal being propagated by the NIO? They obviously shared with constitutional politicians the naive assumption that British strategy towards the north necessarily required the search for some 'solution' in which some accommodation between Unionists and Nationalists was reached. Just as this assumption encouraged the pretensions of the constitutionalists, it also fuelled Provisional hopes that its almost inevitable failure would lead to a fundamental reappraisal of strategy, followed by withdrawal. Their incomprehension of British policy was then compounded by the effects of republican ideology. As Provisional genealogists will point out, the roots of their ideology can be traced back to the late eighteenth-century Protestant separatist, Wolfe Tone. They thus admit more than they realise. For it is clear that, at the basis of their views of the British state and its Irish policies, we have all the simplicities of the Enlightenment. It is a view of the British state that treats it as the instrument of a single-minded and rapacious ruling class. As it was this class's interference in Ireland which wrenched the country from its 'natural' course of development, so too did it possess an almost supernatural capacity to manipulate internal developments in both Irish states. It it thus unsurprising to find that in their reply to the Protestant churchmen who had met leading Provisionals at Feakle, the Provisional Army Council listed as its first demand to the British government: 'The establishment of a constituent assembly elected by the people of Ireland through universal adult suffrage and proportional representation.'[76] If the Provisionals were capable of believing that the British state could at will set to one side the existing structures of the southern state, then very clearly they must have anticipated even fewer problems in the north. Thus, the British state was, according to the Provisional world view, a malevolent demiurge with the capacity to bend all forces to its own will — so long as they were, like the Protestants and the southern client state, of its own making.

The division and demoralisation produced by the Truce and the failure of the withdrawal predictions would lead to the displacement of the O'Connell group from the leadership of the Provisionals. However, the new leadership would soon reveal that its differences with the discredited element extended only to the tactical question of the length of time it would take to force a British withdrawal, and that the essential primitivism of the Provisionals' notions of the nature of British policy would remain unchanged.[77]

The Mason Period

At his first press conference Rees's successor, Roy Mason,

surprised his audience by claiming that his concern over the poor state of the north's economy exceeded any worries he had about the political situation or security: 'Unemployment, little new investment, too many businesses closing down, these are the questions which must receive priority.'[78] In fact since the early seventies the economy of the north had been gripped by a severe industrial crisis. During the 1960s the Northern Ireland economy was fairly dynamic, a product in part of a state-induced diversification of its archaic economic structures.[79] The reversal of this situation in the 1970s was a product of a number of factors — the more general crisis of the United Kingdom economy, the weakening of regional policy, and developments in the textile industry, where many of the branch plants of multi-national companies opened in the late fifties and sixties closed as a result of world recession and competition from cheaper imports.[80] The violence itself obviously had effects in deterring many multi-nationals from considering the north.[81] The result would be a substantial weakening of the industrial structure throughout the decade and a rapidly rising rate of unemployment.

Sectoral Distribution of Northern Ireland Labour Force (%)

	1970		1980	
Agriculture	11.2		9.8	
Manufacturing	31.8	} 47.6	22.6	} 36.1
Other industry (a)	15.8		13.5	
Private services (b)	22.4	} 41.3	25.7	} 54.1
Public services (c)	18.9		28.4	
Total	100.0		100.0	

(a) Construction; mining; transport and communication; gas, electricity and water.
(b) Distribution; banking and finance; miscellaneous services
(c) Professional and scientific; public administration and defence (excluding armed forces).

Source, Bob Rowthorn 'Northern Ireland: an economy in crisis'
Cambridge Journal of Economics 1981

When Mason took over, the unemployment rate, always much

higher than the United Kingdom average, had risen to 10%.[82] A report by four civil servants, published in October 1976, concluded, 'The Northern Ireland economy is in serious difficulty and if no serious measures are taken, the outlook is grim. Unemployment is 10% and on present policies, it is unlikely to fall below that level, whatever upturn there may be in the national economy.'[83] The report also referred, albeit obliquely, to possible negative effects such developments would have on structural inequalities between Protestants and Catholics:

> The characterisitics of a dual economy which Northern Ireland already displays — some areas containing the more dynamic sectors of industry, other areas largely lacking a modern industrial base — will persist. The possibility of removing inequalities of employment and income between the two halves of the economy will become entirely academic . . . The dual nature of the labour market will be perpetuated. The present division between those who are part of the active market and those who are on its margins or outside it altogether will be reinforced.[84]

This crucial recognition of the degree to which a serious economic development strategy for the north would have to take account of the fact that it was precisely Catholics who were over-represented in the marginal areas and sectors of economic activity, would have little serious effect on British state policy in the remaining years of the Labour administration. The Quigley report, although it had suggested various means by which the north might be made more attractive for multi-nationals, considered that, at least in the medium term, reliance on assisted private enterprise was not realistic and opted for *dirigisme*: 'A heavily subsidised Northern Ireland economy, with the state playing a much greater role, both direct and supportive.'[85]

Although Mason was to claim that he had followed the main lines of the report,[86] there is little evidence to support this. If he achieved anything in economic terms it was to shield the north from the worst effects of the deflationary policies followed by the Callaghan government, beginning with the mini-budget of December 1976. This was associated with the sharp increase in the number of people employed in the service sector which took place during the decade. Thus, employment in public servies increased by 52% between 1970 and 79, as compared with 22% in the United Kingdom as a whole.[87] This increase was closely associated with a high and growing dependence of the North's economy on public expenditure. The Quigley Report pointed out that the ratio of public expenditure to GDP was 50% in the United Kingdom and 66% in the north.[88] Although the Labour administration would make much of the degree to which it was financing higher levels of public expenditure per head in the north than elsewhere in the United Kingdom, such complacency could only be supported by the most superficial of analyses. Much of the increase in public expenditure since the war had only served to begin the adjustment of discrepancies between living standards in the north and those in the rest of the United Kingdom.[89] One economist has pointed out that rather than being feather-bedded,

> . . . the degree of social and economic need in Northern Ireland, stemming from higher unemployment, a greater proportion of family dependents, a poorer stock of social capital in housing and health, and lower living standards, was such that the scale of government financial transfers was, until the early 1970s below the level which might have applied if Northern Ireland had 'enjoyed' the scale of spending justified by need.[90]

In practice the economic regime associated with Mason was little more than palliative in its effects. Thus, in a typically exaggerated claim, Mason was to say that a series of economic measures introduced in 1977 had followed the basic lines of the Quigley report.[91] In fact the main proposals were mentioned in the report but it had been made clear that by themselves they would do little to improve the situation.[92] The other aspect of the Mason regime was the significant expenditure entailed in responding to the continuous process of economic and social decline. Already in 1976 the two largest areas of public expenditure were Social Security (23%) and Education and Library (15%) — Law and Order accounted for 11%.[93] Mason and his junior minister Lord Melchett were to be associated with certain forms of ostentatious largesse to local community groups and with the ulitimate 'garlands on chains' — the building throughout the north and particularly in Belfast of a series of leisure centres.[94]

It has been argued that the policy of the British state in this period was characterised by a combination of 'reform and repression.'[95] Such a view greatly exaggerates the positive aspects of the Mason period. In fact, whatever economic and social measures were introduced were a product of a specific political valuation by the NIO. It was clearly felt that, with the end of the cabinet committee's inconsequential search for some final solution, direct rule would have to continue into the forseeable future. However, it was also considered that unalloyed direct rule was 'vulnerable' in that there was a danger that local political forces, angry at their effective expropriation, would mobilise against it. It was therefore necessary to make the direct rule regime less vulnerable by presenting it as 'compassionate and caring'.[96] That the regime's economic and social policies were determined by these quite cynical political calculations also helps explain why Mason consistently refused requests by Gerry Fitt and the Tory Airey Neave for a debate on the Quigley Report in the House of Commons.

In specifically political terms, it was also considered necessary to maintain a public commitment to the establishment of new political institutions in the north.[97] However, it was increasingly obvious that this was little more than a placatory gesture to local politicians, and Mason himself made his satisfaction with the status quo quite clear: 'The majority of people in Northern Ireland want to stay inside the United Kingdom. People feel they get as good a deal out of direct rule as they do out of any other form of rule.'[98] It is clear that Mason's own bumptious and insular arrogance made him relish his role as some sort of governor bringing enlightenment and prosperity to the benighted Irish.[99] Nevertheless, Mason's blustering style was well suited to the Callaghan government's increasingly exiguous relationship to the north. This can only be partly explained by the small and disappearing majority which the Labour Party had in the House of Commons. In 1977 this would lead to negotiations between Michael Foot, in his capacity as Leader of the House, and James Molyneaux, the leader of the Ulster Unionists at Westminster. In return for more seats (Northern Ireland was under represented in population terms at Westminster but up to this point increased representation had been denied by both parties in respose to SDLP and southern pressure that it would represent a move to integration) and some form of 'administrative devolution', it was hoped that the Unionists would support the government.[100] This peculiarly base piece of horse-trading was not simply a reflection of the government's weak parliamentary position. Even a Labour government with a large parliamentary majority, would very probably have behaved no differently. The pre-requisite for a different approach would have been a searching critique of the main characteristics and limitations of the British state's increased involvement since 1969. But as the cabinet committee's deliberations demonstrated, the only even semi-serious thought which that administration was prepared to give to the north concerned possible forms of extrication.

Because it was only possible to improve social and economic conditions to a small degree, and because local politics in Northern Ireland had reached an obvious impasse, Mason began to adopt a slightly theatrical attitude to his own administration, embellishing its essentially pedestrian features through a series of 'confrontations' between himself and the local forces of darkness and unreason. Although the main lines of the state's security policies — particularly the 'primacy' of a modernised and reorganised RUC — had been laid down during Rees's period, Mason was to present them in a particularly crude and brutal manner. At his first press conference he had claimed that the IRA was 'reeling'[101] and he was to follow this with a string of triumphalist statements. Certainly, at the end of 1976 Kenneth Newman, head of the RUC, could report to Mason that complete Provisional units had been eliminated in various parts of the north and that charges against the members of the Provisional had more than doubled compared to 1975.[102] A year later, even a hostile commentator could admit that 'it may be that he has broken the fighting capacity of the Provisional IRA'.[103] Mason was claiming at this time that 'the tide had turned against the terrorists and the message for 1978 is one of real hope.'[104] In fact, 1978 was to see clear signs that the Provisionals had been able to re-group and reorganise. By the end of February, when Provisional fire-bombs incinerated eleven people in a restaurant, there had been over 100 explosions, many of them much larger than had been the case in 1977.[105]

Mason's security policies were clearly no more purposeful than his economic ones. It was not simply that the increasing evidence of the systematic brutalisation of suspects in the RUC's interrogation units was to become extremely embarrassing for the government.[106] At a more general level, the triumphalist tone of the Mason regime was to push constitutional Catholic politics in a more militant nationalist direction. This was something of an achievement given the development of a mass peace movement at the time which had substantial degrees of support amongst the Catholic masses.[107] The progressive potential of this movement was effectively undermined by the state's response to it. Presented as proof that 'normality' was returning, the peace movement was used as a crude ideological weapon against the Provos, whose vehement denunciations of its supposedly pro-British nature were thus confirmed. More cynicism about British policy was encouraged by the discrepancy between Mason's fulsome praise for the virtues of continued direct rule and the government's formal commitment to some form of political settlement based on the accommodation of the 'two traditions.'

However, it was increasingly obvious that all such talk of political movement was based not on any evaluation of changes in the internal balance of forces, but rather on the need to maintain the co-operation of the southern state. In June 1977, the Coalition government which had presided over an economy wracked by its own severe structural problems, exacerbated by the post '73 oil price rise, lost the general election to Fianna Fail, which had focussed its campaign on a doubling of prices and a rapid rise in unemployment under the Coalition. Jack Lynch was now publicly critical of the continuation of direct rule without an initiative.[108] Later in the year, Carter, the US President, under pressure from the Irish-American lobby, had urged an initiative and attached a vague promise of increased American investment.[109] Lynch met Callaghan in London in the autumn and their communiqué referred to the British aim of getting a 'devolved system of government in which all sections of the community could participate.' Lynch claimed that he had been reassured that there would be no drift towards integration.[110]

However, when Mason did produce his response — a 'Five

Point Plan' — it bore a remarkable resemblance to the proposals for administrative devolution which the Unionist leader at Westminster, James Molyneaux, had begun to advocate.[111] Mason presented his plan for partial devolution as an interim stage to the devolution of a legislative body with a whole range of powers.[112] In typical fashion he justified such an interim measure by referring to the 'old-fashioned intransigent attitudes' of the local political parties.[113] But, given these attitudes, it was inconsistent to expect the SDLP to take seriously proposals which an important section of Unionist opinion regarded as very close to their own.[114]

Such inconsistency reflected a central characteristic of the Mason period. This was the discrepancy between, on the one hand, the assertion of strong direction from the direct rule administration and the associated denigration of local political parties and, on the other, the need to hold out some promise of a future return of political power to these very parties. This discrepancy, although most blatantly apparent under Mason, goes to the heart of the strategy of the British state in the period after the introduction of direct rule. Forced to intervene, largely by the disasters produced by a mixture of ignorance and ineptitude, the British ruling class was still preoccupied with limiting the cost of increased involvement. This had meant only the most superficial responses to the profound problems of economic stagnation and differential access to resources, which did much to underpin the reproduction of sectarianism. The lack of a substantive reformist dynamic meant that the objective of relegating local political forces to a largely secondary and passive role inevitably failed. A direct rule regime which treated reform as a largely accomplished fact inevitably ignored the material bases for the continuing articulation of nationalist grievance.

Impasse for the SDLP

The massive Loyalist repudiation of the Sunningdale agreement through the UWC strike was a shattering and demoralising blow to the SDLP. The party's response was to attack the government for failing adequately to support the Executive whilst at the same time demanding that the British state vigorously assert its will in the future. Thus it was proposed that in advance of the elections for the Constitutional Convention the British government should make it clear to the loyalists that power-sharing and an Irish Dimension in the form of agreed North-South institutions were 'non-negotiable.' If the Loyalist population rejected these terms then the British should revoke all their guarantees to the Unionists and declare that 'it will remain in Northern Ireland only until such time as agreed institutions of government are established which allow the people of Ireland, north and south, to live together in harmony and peace.'[115] The notion that the British state had the capacity by threats or action to impel a recasting of Loyalist attitudes has a long and undistinguished history in nationalist discourse. That the leadership of the SDLP turned to it at this juncture was unsurprising. If members of the southern government were now prepared to admit that they had pushed for too much of an Irish Dimension at Sunningdale,[116] the SDLP could only have admitted this by acknowledging the essential barreness of the rest of the agreement and of their whole period 'in office.' This was unlikely as there were serious fears that the party's failure to achieve anything was likely to lead to a drift of its supporters towards the Provisionals.[117] One response to this was to move towards a simple nationalist traditionalism and the demand for a British declaration of intent to withdraw.[118] Apart from the danger represented by ceding crucial ideological ground to the Provisionals, such a development would severely divide the party and damage its image in Britain and Europe as an essentially progressive and modernising force. However in maintaining its main objective — power-sharing and an Irish Dimension —whilst at the same time assigning to the British state the duty to create the conditions for their implementation, the party was simply storing up problems for itself in the future.

Although a boycott of the Convention elections had been considered,[119] the truce and the apparent legitimacy this gave to the Provos ensured that the party took part. The results, which saw the party broadly maintain its position whilst the UUUC effectively hegemonised the Protestant vote[120] on a platform of opposition to power-sharing and an Irish Dimension, appeared to rule out any possibilities of accommodation. However, precisely because the effect of the truce was to generate a degree of apprehension in both blocs about Britain's ultimate intentions, there was for a period an unexpected atmosphere of compromise. The most significant expression of this was the proposal for an emergency coalition put forward by William Craig, who claimed that it had been the SDLP who had originally suggested the idea.[121] However the *volte face* of Paisley, who had originally favoured the notion but who now did his utmost to ensure that it was rejected, saved the party from what would have been an excruciating choice — 'If the idea had been pursued, they would have been forced to choose between the aspiration towards Irish unity and the fact of accepting the permanence of the Ulster state.'[122]

Northern Ireland Convention Election Results 1975

Parties	Votes		Number of Candidates	Number of Seats Won
	Number	Percent		
Loyalists				
Official Unionists	169,797	25.8	27	19
DUP (Paisleyites)	97,073	14.7	18	12
Vanguard	83,507	12.7	17	14
Other Loyalists	10,140	1.5	5	2
Total Loyalist	360,517	64.8	67	47
Alliance party	64,657	9.8	23	8
Unionist party of Northern Ireland	50,891	7.7	18	5
NILP	9,102	1.4	6	1
SDLP	156,049	23.7	30	17
Republican Clubs (Officials)	14,515	2.2	17	0
Independent/others	2,430	0.4	4	0
TOTAL	658,161	100.0	165	78

Source: R. Rose *Northern Ireland: A Time of Choice* (London 1976) p.97

Under Mason the sense in which the SDLP had shared experience of political expropriation with the Loyalists when the truce and the Convention were under way soon disappeared. The sympathy with which the Mason regime was increasingly regarded by the dominant Unionist party, the Official Unionists, and by the Orange Order[123] — together with the move to consider increased representation in the context of the interim devolution proposals — produced a more stridently nationalist response. In August 1977, an SDLP policy committee produced a document which argued for greater emphasis upon the Irish Dimension, in response to what was interpreted as the British policy of drifting towards integration.[124] It was this document and the SDLP's adoption of it which was to lead to the eventual expulsion from the party of Paddy Devlin, one of the few elements in its leadership with an urban and labourist background.[125] The party faced more problems in October with the formation of the Irish Independence Party, which was in effect composed of 'constitutional' Provisionals, and which concentrated its attacks upon the incapacity of the SDLP and demanded a British declaration of intent.[126] The *Irish Times* Northern correspondent noted the significance of these developments: 'Many in the SDLP hold views remarkably close to the IIP, the IIP is a sign of an apparently inexorable shift of opinion within the minority and within the SDLP away from the idea that it is possible to work within the present Northern Ireland state to achieve their long term objective of Irish unity.[127] Of course, it had not been part of British strategy to consider the unlikely eventuality of gradual elimination of partition. Instead it had been hoped that a growing familiarity with the realities of a situation in which they played a subordinate role (with the Unionists) in running the north would have allowed the SDLP leadership gradually to accustom their supporters to working within the northern state. However, the defeat of the Executive left the SDLP blithely unaware of the role they were expected to play and with their aspirations unaltered. The very 'unconstitutional' way in which the Executive was destroyed allowed the illusions of the party to remain unaffected. Two years in office would have clearly demonstrated to the party and its supporters the strict limitations on what it was possible to achieve in the way of their ultimate objectives. It might have even provoked a serious and productive split. As it was the real problems associated with its strategy were blamed upon 'Loyalist intransigence' and British 'lack of will.' An explanation of this sort could not help but lead to a resurgence of traditional nationalism.

Mason's arrogance and his obvious lack of sympathy for the SDLP simply exacerbated this tendency. By the beginning of 1978 the party indicated that a further hardening of line was necessary, in order to emphasise that it was 'the British dimension which is an obstacle keeping us away from a lasting solution.'[128] John Hume, the deputy leader, was one of those acutely aware of the dangers of being manoeuvred into a position from which all one could do was to demand withdrawal. He was completely incapable however of doing more than produce superficially new and attractive versions of what were in fact traditional nationalist notions. This is the significance of his ponderous adumbration of a 'third way' between the status quo and a demand for a declaration of intent — the notion of an 'Agreed Ireland': 'The third option open to the British government is to declare that its objective in Ireland is the bringing together of both Irish traditions in reconciliation and agreement.'[129] The verbal sleight of hand by which notions of reconciliation and agreement simply serve to obscure the central and traditional notion — that the British state has the capacity and obligation to create the conditions in which Protestant consent would be forthcoming — was to be the insubstantial basis for Hume's elevation to the level of 'statesman' in the next five years.

The Limits of Paisleyism

The 'Protestant backlash' which destroyed the power-sharing executive was clearly an enigmatic phenomenon for many commentators. Neal Ascherson, who had been in Belfast during the UWC strike, was one of many who were surprised by the radicalism of the ideas being expressed by some prominent paramilitary leaders: 'The UDA is only one of the sources of a fountain of radical ideas which clearly terrify the more traditionally minded bodies dedicated to maintaining Protestant supremacy.' He was obviously so entranced that he informed his readers that its leader, Andy Tyrie, 'has a surprising resemblance to the novelist Gunter Grass.'[130]

No one would dispute the naive nature of much discussion in these circles for, as Ascherson pointed out, Protestant supporters of independence '(were) inventing a Catholic population eager to abandon Republicanism and the Irish Dimension for the sake of a reborn Ulster.'[131] Yet the significance of Protestant para-militarism lay less in the undoubted support for some form of 'independent Ulster' solution which was expressed, but rather in the very fact that serious political discussion took place, discussion which was predicated upon an insistence that no return to pre-1969 conditions was possible. The UDA's paper had informed its readership before the strike that opposition to the Executive did not mean that power-sharing was to be ruled out in all circumstances:

> The present arrangement in the Northern Ireland Assembly is not power-sharing. It is government by appointment . . . Power-sharing is anathema to some of our people but unless you go for a Protestant Ulster for a Protestant people — that is you exclude the Roman Catholics, if they are not willing to go then they will have to be pushed out, it is difficult to see how you can get around the issue.[132]

The same paper argued later, after the strike, that the fragmentation of Protestant politics into seven parties was a progressive development.[133] This was just one indication of how a significant current of popular Protestantism did not hanker after the 'good old days' of monolithic Unionism.

However, such sentiments expressed only one line within the group which had led the strike. As its most sensitive historian has put it,

> Dissension and fragmentation were almost inevitable as soon as decisions had to be taken about where to go next. The UWC had never existed as a coherent organisation with a political pro-gramme; originally a tiny group of key workers, it really became a mere label for all the groups who hastily responded to the daily demands of the strike.[134]

Nelson describes the various tendencies as follows: 'The UWC contained hardline Loyalists, more conciliatory, socially radical elements and people who had just not thought what constructive alternative they were aiming for.' Glen Barr, a Derry trade unionist who had been a prominent and articulate member of the UWC, together with some leading members of the para-military UVF, saw the UWC as the possible basis for the develop-ment of an independent, working-class political grouping.[135] However, the tendency which would in the end dominate both the UWC and the UDA was that which favoured support for Paisley and the DUP in their increasingly obvious struggle with the Official Unionists. It is important, nevertheless, that the increasingly significant role of the DUP in Protestant politics be carefully analysed. It is facile and superficial to argue that, 'what Paisley has done is split the Protestant community along lines which approximate to sociological class divisions. Unfortun-ately, while the Protestant workers have broken the chains that bound them to their upper-class leaders, they have broken to the right.'[136] In fact what is most noticeable about the development of the DUP in this period is its relatively late arrival in the heart-lands of the Protestant urban proletariat. As an ex-Paisleyite put it,

> In the late sixties it was commonplace for left wing writers on the growing crisis in Ulster to represent the embryonic Protestant Unionist party of the Rev Ian Paisley as a populist movement destined to capture and articulate the latent resentments of the Protestant working class in Belfast. Yet a political breakthrough in Belfast eluded Paisley's party. In fact such a breakthrough was to come first in rural Ulster.[137]

The main reason for the DUP's only very partial influence on the Protestant working class was strategic. For, despite Paisley's undisguised and consuming desire for domination in Protestant politics, and the relatively favourable conditions created by the divided and demoralised state of the Official Unionists, the DUP's commitment to the return of 'strong' devolved institu-tions — a coded reference to pre-1969 conditions — was to force it first into futile confrontations with the British state and, sub-sequently, into an over-eager commitment to the increasingly cosmetic series of Tory initiatives.

Paisleyism reflected all the narrowness of the rural and small town bourgeois and petty-bourgeois evangelicals who pre-dominated in its leadership and party structure, and the height of its ambition would have been the capture of state institutions at both local and provincial level, in order to 'defend Ulster' from the secularist and 'materialist' tide that had overwhelmed the rest of the United Kingdom. The continuation of direct rule was thus intolerable to the DUP, for without local political institutions its politics could not achieve real or distinct expression. Insofar as *Paisley* was able to act as a hegemonic force in Protestant politics, in situations of crisis, it was because he could embody most adequately the spirit of stubborn and embattled resisitance to some apparent threat to the Union. However the DUP, and this was the fatal contradiction, was committed as a party to a militant struggle for a type of devolution which it was apparent no British government would countenance. The inevitable confrontation led to widespread fears — particularly amongst the working class — that Paisley and his supporters would contemplate an open confrontation with Britain, which could result in British disengagement and a total collapse of the North's state-supported economy.

The Loyalist strike of 1977 illustrates the contradictions of Paisleyism most clearly. The key role which Paisley had played in mobilising all varieties of Unionist representatives in the Convention against Craig's proposals for emergency coalition with the SDLP had served both to establish Paisley's public predominance and, by hastening the disintegration of the Vanguard Party, to create further preconditions for the growth of the DUP.[138] Perceiving the diminished stature of the Unionist Party in the period after direct rule, Paisley embarked on a direct attempt to marginalise it. It is conceivable that Paisley was influenced here by a misreading of the policies of the British state; that (ironically, like the Provos) he interpreted the Truce and the Convention as signs of indeterminacy which would allow the success of a forceful assertion of traditional demands. In 1976, Paisley and Peter Robinson — the DUP leader in East Belfast —entered into renewed contact with the UDA. Subsequently, a United Unionist Action Council was formed from the DUP, from sections of Vanguard which had opposed Craig and from remnants of the UWC and UDA. The alliance aimed to use strike action–enforced by the UDA — to force the British government to implement the majority (Loyalist) report of the Convention and to adopt harsher security measures.[139] The strike was launched on 3 May 1977 and had collapsed miserably within ten days. The differences with 1974 were patent. Although the Action Council had claimed that the government was attempting 'to destroy the traditional Unionist conception of the Union,'[140] the prevailing political conditions did little to make such claims popular. If there had still been the fears, widespread in 1975, that Britain intended to withdraw, the situation would have been radically different. However, Mason and the NIO had the advantage of a detailed report, drafted by the Orange Order, on the question of withdrawal. Having dismissed such fears as groundless, the report went on to comment on the favourable position of Unionism, 'On every side there is growing acceptance of the Ulster case for increased representation in the Commons . . . In the absence of a devolved government here Westminster has apparently accepted her responsibility to govern, and if Mr Mason's remarks are to be believed, the intention is to govern well.'[141]

When the Official Unionists condemned the strike as posing a real threat to the Union, they were clearly responding to the increasing evidence that Protestants were willing to accept direct rule, if the alternative was to be open confrontation with the British state.[142] Paisley's inability to convince the Protestant masses that such a confrontation was necessary clearly demonstrated the less than hegemonic capacity of DUP strategy. Paisleyism had grown in direct response to the burgeoning crisis of the Unionist state in the late 1960s, when it had represented itself as the resolute response to republicanism, British duplicity and the Unionist Party's vacillations and compromises. The continuation of the Provisionals' campaign and the necessary ambiguities of British policy after direct rule would always ensure a substantial reservoir of support for Paisley. However the period culminating in Sunningdale had seen the Official Unionist Party rid itself of its 'compromisers' — the Faulknerites — and although the party was itself to remain divided over strategy, the major strategic division in Protestant politics no longer ran between the two parties, as they were both committed to the kind of return of devolved institutions envisaged in the Convention Report. If the DUP could justifiably attack the OUP for lack of unity or resolution on prosecuting a devolution strategy, the Unionists could continue to rely on the unwillingness of the predominant sections of the Protestant bourgeoisie and proletariat to support devolution once it threatened a crisis in relations with the British state. The strategic disarray within the Offical Unionists — the open divisions between 'devolutionists' and 'integrationists' — was an obvious source of weakness in electoral competition for a party which stressed its ability to provide, 'strong' leadership. However, the very divisions in Official Unionism reflected real dilemmas and contradictions in Protestant politics which Paisleyism was incapable of resolving.

The classical forms of Ulster Unionist unity (1892-93, 1910-14, 1920-21) had been created in periods when substantial recastings of the relationship between the British state and Ireland had seemed plausible. The crucial factor about the present phase of 'Troubles' was that the crisis of the Unionist state did not in reality presage any such recasting — despite the manifold delusions to which it had given rise. The Ulster Unionist party was only able to maintain the unity of its period of state formation through its control of the state apparatuses — acquiesced in by London. When this was removed in 1972, not as a prelude to a 'final solution' to the Irish question but rather to a more effective central control of the province — the basis for a subsequent hegemonic Unionist party was removed. However Paisleyism itself could only rather pathetically parody the past 'heroic' phases of Unionist resistance. Whilst it was capable of establishing itself as a substantial force in Protestant politics, it was profoundly incapable of attracting the core elements of the Protestant bourgeoisie, the professional stratum and the working class. It was precisely these elements which, for predominantly instrumental reasons, were prepared to accept direct rule and reject Paisleyism because it was seen as threatening harmonious relations with the British state — on which their own continued reproduction as economic classes was dependent.

The strike also demonstrated the increasing fragmentation of those paramilitary forces which had for a time appeared to be moving towards the radical political option of negotiated independence. The Ulster Loyalist Central Co-Ordinating Committee, set up after the UWC strike to bring together the main Protestant paramilitary groups, had made a declaration in support of independence in 1976. This seemed to some to presage a significant shift in Protestant politics. However, even at the time the only serious observer of Protestant paramilitaries warned against exaggerating the importance of such developments. As she pointed out, much of the impetus for these discussions came from the belief, common in the two years after the 1974 strike, that British withdrawal was inevitable in the near future.[143] The very nature of paramilitary organisations, with their emphasis on hierarchy and military discipline, meant that discussion of these issues was confined to small minorities and even within them there were massive divergences over the social and economic context of independence and, most critically, over the role of Catholics.[144]

The UDA, the major group, although Andy Tyrie, its 'Supreme Commander', was sympathetic to the idea,[145] had withdrawn from the ULCC in 1976 in protest at other members discussing independence with 'Republicans.'[146] The organisation then moved in support of Paisley and the proposal for another strike. As it became clear that British withdrawal was not being seriously considered, support for independence inevitably receded. After the collapse of the strike the leadership of the UDA began to consider the idea more seriously, and over the next two years this was to have the undoubtedly progressive effect of forcing a section of the paramilitary leadership to begin to contemplate the need for some form of accommodation with the nationalists. However, it was precisely the massive difficulties involved in eliciting any sympathetic response from either the SDLP or the 'new style' Provos that made independence a strategic chimera, whatever its undoubted 'civilising' effect on the UDA.

NOTES

1. The *Times* 1 June 1974.
2. Ibid, 4 June 1974.
3. The Northern Ireland Constitution cmnd 5675 (London 1974) p. 8.
4. Ibid, p. 16.
5. The *Times* 5 June 1974.

6. In an article describing an Oxford conference at which some of the key figures in the UWC had participated, Keith Kyle, a journalist and broadcaster with a long-standing interest in Ireland argued that there was a real possibility of a radical change in Protestant working-class consciousness thus making a political settlement much easier to envisage. *Times* 10 July 1974. Fisk, p. 231. According to Fisk, the UWC men 'eagerly' spent their time talking to Irish and British cabinet ministers, including Rees and Orme. Kyle was the latest in a long line of commentators sympathetic to nationalism who have consistently misunderstood the nature of Protestant populism.

7. The nineteenth century mansion on the north Down coast near Belfast which was regarded as a more appropriate location for meetings between officials and paramilitaries than the main centre for government at Stormont.

8. A Labour Junior Minster, Don Concannon, referred to the Convention as a 'cooling off period', in an interview with one of the authors. Keith Kyle pointed out of the various discussion documents prepared for the Convention, the decision to employ a panel of expert advisers and the suggestion that members should take trips abroad to study other 'divided societies': 'All this was clearly intended to take some time.' 'Ulster: The Real Choice' *The Listener* 8 May 1975.

9. The existence of this committee only emerged in 1983, after Tony Benn had written an article in the *Guardian* claiming that during his membership of the cabinet the option of withdrawal was never considered. This was then repudiated by Rees in a letter which revealed the existence of the committee for the first time. (Julia Langdon, 'Labour thought of Ulster pull-out '*Guardian* 19 July 1983). It was clearly the discussions of this committee which allowed the NIO officials to point out to the Provisionals the open-mindedness of the government regarding 'ultimate solutions.' In July, the *Guardian's* Belfast correspondent summed up the situation: 'Constitutionally, politically and militarily, the situation in Northern Ireland has never been so fluid or open to speculation. So-called solutions like independence, restored majority rule, and British withdrawal are openly canvassed and debated in the best informed circles, and with every day that passes the wilder predictions are growing more credible.' Derek Brown, 'The Treacherous Truce' *Guardian* 15 July 1975.

10. *New Stateman* 14 January 1977.

11. Lord Melchett, a Labour Junior Minister under Mason, recalled a conversation with the head of the NIO on the withdrawal issue. Melchett was informed that 'all that would happen would be that the local Protestant power structure would take over.' Author's interview.

12. *Times* 17 September 1974.

13. Ibid, 14 October 1974.

14. Compare the February election; see M Wallace, *British Government in Northern Ireland* (London 1982) p. 125.

15. *Times* 13 October 1974.

16. Ibid 17 October 1974.

17. *Irish Times* 2 November 1974.

18. John Whale and Chris Ryder, 'Ulster 1968-78 A Decade of Despair', *Sunday Times* 18 June 1978.

19. *Irish Republican Information Service* (IRIS) 31 May 1974.

20. Ibid, 19 June 1974.

21. *Republican News* 22 June 1974.

22. Ibid, 3 August 1974.

23. *Irish News* 3 July 1974.

24. Ibid, 8 August 1974.

25. Ibid, 13 July 1976.

26. Ibid, 28 June 1976.

27. *IRIS* 17 July 1974.

28. Ibid, 12 June 1974.

29. Ibid, 10 July 1974.

30. *IRIS* 14 August 1974.

31. E Gallagher and S Worrall, *Christians in Ulster 1968-1980* (Oxford 1982) p. 97.

32. House of Commons *Debates* vol 884, No. 44, 14 January 1975, cols 201-203.

33. Gallagher and Worrall, p. 100.

34. When in September the *Daily Telegraph* carried a front page story that police who had arrested O'Connell in Dublin had recovered a twelve point peace deal, Rees went to the length of issuing a denial through a junior minister in the House of Lords. House of Lords *Official Report* Fifth Series vol 364, September 1975 cols 89-90. However, the statement did admit it was aware of the existence of twelve points, denying that it had agreed to them. In fact there is clear evidence that some at least of the twelve points were in operation. (Mr Paddy Devlin, who had acted as an early intermediary in talks between Provos and NIO, provided a copy of the twelve points dated 11 February 1975). 1. Release of 100 detainees within two to three weeks; 2. phasing out of internment within a specific period; 3. effective withdrawal to barracks meaning three to four thousand troops returned to Britain within six months; 4. an end of system of arrests and screening and large scale searching of Catholic areas; 5. establishment of incident centres — manned by Sinn Fein members and connected with an incident room at Stormont to monitor the ceasefire; 6. provision for 'army to army' discussions at local level; 7. an end of military check points and road blocks at the edges of Catholic areas; 8. immunity from arrest for specific persons; 9. firearms licenses for specific persons; 10. no immediate attempt to introduce the RUC and UDR into Catholic areas; 11. a formal ceasefire agreement to be drawn up by Britain; 12. further talks to take place between IRA leaders and senior British representatives.

35. House of Commons *Debates* vol 884, col 53, 28 February 1975.

36. The *Times* 1 October 1975.

37. *Fortnight* 7 March 1975 and R Fisk 'Rees's Deadly Ceasefire' *New Statesman* 22 August 1975.

38. House of Commons *Debates* vol 897 No 174, col 413, 7 August 1975.

39. *New Statesman* 24 August 1975.

40. *New Statesman* 30 May 1975.

41. John Whale and Chris Ryder, 'Ulster 1968-78 A Decade of Despair' *Sunday Times* 18 June 1978.

42. *Irish Times* 9 June 1978.

43. R Rose, Northern Ireland *A Time of Choice* (London 1976) p. 126.

44. See his reply to question from Biggs Davison, House of Commons *Debates* vol 891 col 628-629, 15 May 1975.

45. House of Commons *Debates* vol 891 col 629, 15 May 1975.

46. House of Commons *Debates* vol 895 col 41, 21 July 1975.

47. *Times* 23 September 1975.

48. *Times* 10 October 1975.

49. W D Flackes, *Northern Ireland A Political Directory 1968-79* (Dublin and New York 1980) p. 117.

50. Vincent Browne 'The Provos settle down for a 20 year war' *Magill* August 1982.

51. *Sunday Times* 19 January 1975.

52. *IRIS* 21 February 1975.

53. *Irish News* 27 February 1975.
54. *IRIS* 28 February 1975.
55. *Irish News* 17 March 1975.
56. *Irish News* 17 February 1975 and 24 March 1975.
57. *Irish News* 28 July 1975.
58. *Irish News* 30 July 1975.
59. *Irish News* 17 November 1975.
60. *Hibernia* 25 July 1975.
61. *Fortnight* 23 January 1976.
62. *Irish News* 11 November 1975.
63. *Irish News* 14 August 1975.
64. *Irish News* 15 August 1975.
65. *Irish News* 23 September 1975.
66. *Hibernia* 31 October 1975.
67. *Irish News* 7 January 1976. O'Brady asked the Feakle clergymen to intervene in an attempt to restore the truce.
68. *Irish Times* 12 January 1976.
69. *Irish News* 19 and 23 March 1976.
70. One leading member of PSF warned 'the enemy within is the most dangerous' *Irish News* 20 April 1976
71. A senior member of the NIO at the time saw the Truce as a means of getting rid of internment — 'a noose round the neck of the government' and of perhaps dividing the political element from the 'militarists' — interview with one of authors.
72. A Labour colleague of Rees referred to his capacity to waffle as his major virtue. (Interview with one of authors). His own political adviser was to openly admit the facade nature of Rees's period: 'Merlyn and I hadn't a clue where we were going.' Interview with one of authors.
73. House of Commons *Debates* vol 913, 14 June 1976, col 50
74. *Ibid* vol 914, 2 July 1976 cols 879-883
75. *Ibid* vol 913, 14 June 1976, col 44
76. *Text of reply from the Provisional Army Council to the proposal handed by the Protestant Churchmen to the Sinn Fein representatives at the meeting at Feakle last week.* The authors would like to thank Paddy Devlin for providing us with a copy of this document.
77. Thus Danny Morrison — often portrayed as one of the two main representatives of a modernised, progressive and politically sophisticated Provisionalism justified the bombing of the Grand Hotel, Brighton during the Conservative Party conference — 'If that bomb had killed the British Cabinet, examine then what would have happened. There would have been a rethink within British political circles and it probably would have led to a British withdrawal in a much shorter period. It would have been unique in British constitutional history, apart maybe from Guy Fawkes' *Observer* 14 October 1984. Apart from the ignorant failure to note the predominantly integrative effect of his historical example, this statement demonstrates the practical effects of their particular view of the British state — its policies are conceived as product of interests of a ruling clique — hurt the clique and the policies will inevitably change. That the clique is circumscribed by any objective determinants apart from its own appetites is effectively denied.
78. The *Times* 28 September 1976.
79. This diversification took place against a secular decline in the north's three main staples:

	1950	1973
Agriculture, forestry and fishing	101,000	55,000
Textiles	65,000	19,000
Shipbuilding	24,000	10,000

Northern Ireland: Finance and Economy: Discussion Paper, Northern Ireland Office (London 1974) p. 6

80. Rowthorn, p. 8.
81. Over the period 1966-71 British and foreign multi-nationals set up 51 new manufacturing units in Northern Ireland and created 11,600 new jobs. Over 1972-76 they set up a mere 15 units and created only 900 jobs. Ibid, p. 9.
82. *Belfast Telegraph* 11 October 1974.
83. *Economic and Industrial Strategy for Northern Ireland Report by Review Team* Belfast HMSO 1976 p. 66.
84. Ibid.
85. Ibid, p. 25.
86. *Irish Times* 2 August 1977. One of his junior ministers, Don Concannon put it even more floridly — 'Quigley was my bible.' Interview with one of the authors.
87. Rowthorn, p. 11.
88. *Quigley*, p. 58.
89. J Simpson 'Economic Development: Cause or Effect' in J Dabry, p. 93.
90. Ibid, p. 94.
91. *Irish Times* 2 August 1977.
92. The main proposals were a writing off of £250 million debt of the NI Electricity Service aimed at cutting industrial costs and an increase in almost every incentive available to local and incoming industry. Ibid and *Fortnight* August 1977. A closer reading of the government's statement shows that it goes only a very small way to meet the needs which the Quigley report identified.'
93. *Quigley*, p. 59.
94. For contrasting uncritical and realistic assessments of Melchett's role see Mary Holland *New Statesman* 22 July 1977 and Paddy Murphy *Hibernia* 18 February 1978
95. See *Workers Research Unit* (Belfast) Bulletin No. 2 Winter 1977
96. Lord Melchett made these calculation clear in an interview with one of the authors. See also, I Fallon and J Srodes *De Lorean* (London 1983).
97. *Times* 27 November 1976.
98. *Irish Times* 6 November 1976.
99. He was obviously personally committed to a view of the basically unreasonable nature of the Irish. See *Irish Times* 17 January 1977
100. *Times* 23 March 1977.
101. *Times* 28 September 1976.
102. P Taylor, *Beating the Terrorists?* (London 1980) pp. 80-81.
103. *New Statesman* 6 January 1978.
104. *Irish Times* 30 December 1977.
105. *Hibernia* 23 February 1978: 'last autumn's deceptive lull was a period of calculated and determined reorganisation . . . .'
106. The best account of this is in Taylor, ibid.
107. See K Kelly, pp. 252-7.
108. *Times* 20 June 1977.
109. *New Statesman* 11 May 1977.

110. *Irish Times* 29 September 1977.

111. *Irish Times* 14 December 1976.

112. House of Commons *Debates* vol 939, col 1727, 24 November 1977.

113. Ibid, col 1727.

114. Molyneux was able to quote from an article written by Mason in *Socialist Commentary* to establish the similarity of positions. House of Commons *Debates* vol 957, 9 November 1978, col 1167.

115. *Irish Times* 4 September 1974.

116. Downey ibid, p. 140.

117. *Irish News* 2 June 1974.

118. Hugh Logue, an Assemblyman, demanded this; *Irish News* 3 and 7 June 1974.

119. *Irish News* 7 December 1974.

120. See table overleaf.

121. See interview with Robin Day, *The Listener* 15 January 1976.

122. McAlister, p. 160.

123. See a very pro-Mason statement *Irish Times* 23 February 1977.

124. *Irish Times* 12 and 15 August 1977.

125. *Irish Times* 26 August 1977 and 19 September 1977.

126. Ibid, 8 October 1977.

127. Ibid, 5 November 1977.

128. Ibid, 7 February 1978.

129. *Irish Times* 16 February 1978.

130. *Observer* 2 June 1974.

131. Ibid.

132. *Ulster Loyalist* 14 March 1974.

133. Ibid 4 July 1974.

134. Sarah Nelson 'Ulster's Uncertain Defenders: A Study of Protestant Politics 1969-75' University of Strathclyde, PhD 1980 p. 470

135. Ibid, 472.

136. Bell, *The British in Ireland* p. 62.

137. *Irish Times* 8 May 1979.

138. Smyth, pp. 100-104.

139. Ibid, p. 112.

140. Ibid, p. 117.

141. *Irish Times* 23 February 1977.

142. NOP Polls recorded 51% of Protestants and 48% of Catholics in favour of continued direct rule in March 1974. The corresponding figures in March 1976 were 72% and 79% See R Rose, I McAlister and P Mair 'Is there a concurring majority about Northern Ireland?' *Studies in Public Policy no. 22* University of Strathclyde, Glasgow 1978.

143. Sarah Nelson, 'The New Independence Debate' *Fortnight* 3 December 1976

144. Sarah Nelson 'Independence: Strategies for Action' *Fortnight* 13 February 1977 and Bill Rolston 'Independence and the Dependent State' *Fortnight* 1 April 1977

145. 'Profile of Andy Tyrie', *Fortnight* 19 March 1976

146. W D Flackes, *Northern Ireland: A Political Directory 1968-74* (Dublin and New York 1980) p. 137.

4

From the Hunger Strike to the Forum Report

The Atkins Initiative

During the campaign which took Mrs Thatcher into power in May 1979, the INLA had murdered the Conservatives' principal Northern Irish spokesman, Airey Neave; after her victory, Thatcher appointed Humphrey Atkins as the new Secretary of State for Northern Ireland. The Conservative election manifesto had contained one significant innovation: 'In the absence of devolved government we seek to establish one or more elected regional councils with a wide range of powers over local services.' This proposal was clearly based on integrationist and minimalist assumptions. However, in the absence of Neave, whose brainchild it was, no serious attempt was made to implement this policy.[1] Atkins at first hesitated; in July he told the House of Commons there was still too much disagreement between the two political traditions in Northern Ireland for him 'even to begin to suggest the possible shape of an acceptable structure of government for the province.'[2] In June Ian Paisley's massive personal triumph in the European elections, combined with the moderate Alliance Party's relatively poor showing, seemed further reason to tread warily. Paisley, who had been forced to call off the 1977 strike because of lack of support, received almost 30% of the vote — very much more than the 10.2% his party had received at the general election in May 1979. Paisley's electoral success brought closer the moment of truth for his strategy: to succeed it would necessitate British state willingness to contemplate a massive Catholic withdrawal from constitutional politics. Even the impetuous Mrs Thatcher might reasonably have been expected to hesitate before such a prospect.

A number of separate events then forced the British government to act. Earl Mountbatten and his party were assassinated on 27 August; eighteen British soldiers were massacred on the same day, at Warrenpoint. A number of sectarian murders of Catholics followed. Internationally, there was an intensification of American pressure, orchestrated by Speaker O'Neill, Senators Kennedy and Moynihan, and Governor Carey. This culminated, in British eyes, in the decision at the end of August 1979 by the American state department to suspend the sale of handguns to the RUC. As Adrian Guelke has argued: 'This was an alarming development for the British government. Historically, American Presidents had successfully resisted far greater domestic political pressure over the Irish question than Carter faced.'[3]

Obviously, the developments which generated the mood for a new initiative were profoundly contradictory. At first, the American pressure appeared to be decisive: on 16 September, Sir Nicholas Henderson, the British ambassador to the United States, announced in Washington that Atkins was embarking on a political initiative.[4] The Thatcher government seems to have made little attempt to evaluate critically this American pressure.[5] Instead, the somewhat flustered Atkins was propelled towards a new initiative. He announced that he would be calling a conference of interested parties in order to discuss possible paths to devolution. The Prime Minister told the *New York Times* that she was in a mood to impose a solution: 'We will listen for a while. We hope we will get agreement. But then the government will have to make some decisions and say, having listened to everyone, we are going to try this or that, whichever we get most support for.'[6] But, the initiative designed originally to fob off Irish American pressure, took on very different colours in Northern Ireland. Describing the objective of the Prime Minister's strategy, such as it was, Peter Jenkins wrote in February 1980: 'There will be a return to something very like majority rule but hedged around with blocking devices, checks and balances, appeals procedures and constitutional guarantees.'[7]

In accordance with this, the British government published a

consultative document in November 1979. Its objective was stated to be 'the highest level of agreement . . . which will best meet the immediate needs of Northern Ireland.'[8] Discussion on Irish unity, confederation, independence or the constitutional status of Ulster was ruled out of order, and an appendix containing six illustrative models of systems of government was added to stimulate the participants. The White Paper explicitly declared that direct rule was not a 'satisfactory' basis for the government of the province. The White Paper's premises also ruled out any discussion of the 'Irish dimension.' The immediate effect was to provoke a split within the SDLP and the resignation of its leader, Gerry Fitt, who favoured continued dialogue with Unionists even under its restrictive condition. The party leadership was assumed by John Hume, a politician supported by the majority of party activists, who regarded this exclusion of the Irish dimension as quite intolerable.

In his resignation statement on 22 November 1979, Fitt declared: 'Nationalism has been a political concept in Ireland over many, many years but I suggest that it has never brought peace to the people of the six counties. I for one have never been a nationalist to the total exclusion of my socialist ideals.'[9] However, Fitt's attempt to raise this fundamental issue of principle was ignored, owing to the widely held, though somewhat dubious view that, whilst Hume was a 'skilful and mature strategist', Fitt was best characterised by his 'fast talking, Tammany Hall style.'[10] Despite his opposition to violence, it was argued that Hume knew that 'the history of Anglo-Irish relations shows that those Irish politicians who have fared best in dealing with Britain are those who have made it clear that the men of violence, the mob even, are waiting on the sidelines.'[11] Such an explicit analogy with Parnell[12] was — despite the support it has received from Sorel[13] — a misleading one; terrorism had never been anything other than an embarrassment to Parnell, and his extra-parliamentary strength was based on complex, sometimes militant, but predominantly legal forms of class struggle.[14] But of one thing there would be little doubt; Hume's accession to the leadership of the SDLP marked the advent of a more nationalist mood in the party as a whole and bode ill for the Atkins initiative.

The course of the Atkins initiative was a consistently erratic one. Given Paisley's huge personal triumph in the European elections, it became necessary to insist — not for the first time — that this particular monster had been tamed, whilst his principal opponents within the Protestant block, the Official Unionists, were vilified. Paisley 'in private' connived at this impression to some degree. He described Atkins as his 'friend', and the 'engaging mannerly Tory'[15] who had been expected to appeal at the personal level (more particularly to the SDLP), thus became the first Secretary of State to earn this sobriquet. Paisley ignored the Atkins conference working paper's discussion (paragraphs 32 and 33) of power-sharing; he even ignored Atkins's climbdown, under SDLP pressure, in allowing the 'Irish dimension' to be discussed at the conference.[16] But it was clear that Paisley's objective remained a majority rule devolved government; for a brief moment it seemed as if he was at one with the British government on this point.[17] He became the object of compliments which would have turned the head of a more susceptible politician. 'It's because he smells power that he is a totally changed man', said a senior official in London.[18] 'Paisley's always been a wrecker but now he is trying to build something', noted one of the Northern Ireland Office officials.[19] The *Economist* observed in February 1980 'Mr Paisley seems to be becoming more moderate now that he sees the possibility of becoming top dog in the province.'[20]

Meanwhile, the Official Unionists who refused to support the Atkins initiative were both castigated and underestimated. Molyneux, it was said, lacks 'grassroots support' because he is on the 'integrationist' wing of his party — 'those who do not complain about continuing direct rule from Westminster and who would like Ulster to be linked more closely to London, as Scotland and Wales are.'[21] Peter Jenkins observed contemptuously of the OUP: 'their party still continues to disintegrate with the help of Enoch Powell; "the baddies and the thickies" as one observer unkindly put it, are coming to the fore!'[22] But by June 1980 such optimism had evaporated entirely. The *Economist* commented 'Mr Paisley is not a born again moderate. He will not tolerate shares for Catholics in any assembly. He is not going to accept anything less than full Protestant majority rule.'[23] It was even acknowledged that a Tory Prime Minister could hardly ride roughshod over the wishes of the OUP. In accordance with this new realism, doubts began to surface about the value of the whole operation. At first there was a clear insistence that: 'The lack of a political forum deprives Ulster's young politicians of a place to ripen their ideas, make their names and push out their worn out elders.'[24] But, a month later an editorial in the same journal acknowledged that the 'canny Ulsterman' might well be saying: 'We prefer to go on being ruled directly by London and to go on drawing lots of subsidies from London as now. The desire of ordinary people for new local government is usually less burning than local politicians assume.'[25] By November, Thatcher's cabinet committee formally admitted the collapse of the Atkins initiative.[26] It had never come remotely within sight of achieving its objectives and it is difficult to avoid the conclusion that the confused and incoherent strategic thinking which had accompanied it deserved no better reward.

A temporary diversion was provided by the talks with the British and Irish Prime Ministers in Dublin in December 1980. Like Paisley, the British perception of Haughey had changed dramatically during the year. In February, Peter Jenkins wrote in the *Guardian*: 'Mr Charlie Haughey, the new man in Dublin with his impeccable Republican credentials, has the authority to exercise tougher controls at the border and over the illegal activities of the IRA in the south. His impact is already noticeable.'[27] But again by July the mood was soon to become more sober and pessimistic: 'Mr Haughey has dashed early hopes that his supergreen (nationalist, pro-unification) credentials would allow him to find a solution for the north. Instead, Mr Haughey now seems afraid that he is not green enough.'[28] Haughey indeed made an attempt to remove the 'admirably anti-IRA' Irish ambassador from Washington and became 'the first Dublin prime minister of recent times to refuse to condemn IRA front organisations in the United States.'[29]

Under these circumstances Haughey did remarkably well at the Dublin talks. Thatcher, piqued by the failure of the Atkins initiative, seems to have been unusually open to the Irish Prime Minister's persuasive powers. In their joint communiqué after the talks of 8 December 1980 Thatcher acknowledged Britain's 'unique relationship' with Ireland; she permitted the establishment of joint study groups to find ways of expressing this uniqueness in 'new institutional structures.' The two Prime Ministers decided to devote the next of their twice yearly meetings to 'special consideration' of the totality of relationships within these islands. Haughey's subsequent demagogic exploitation of this vague and mysterious phrase both mobilised Paisleyites and angered Thatcher, who had intended no more than a cosmetic concession. On 11 December, Thatcher assured Paisley that she had conceded nothing. But the ambiguity remained until at least 18 March 1981, when Brian Lenihan, the Irish foreign minister, pathetically acknowledged that Northern Ireland's constitutional position had not been discussed at the Dublin summit. By this time, however, Paisley had already made the decision to launch a major mobilisation of disorientated Loyalists. In truth, the inconsistencies and incoherence of Britain's publicly proclaimed policy bear much of the responsibility for this mishap. The integrationist ethos of the Conservative election manifesto had been buried without discussion, and there had clearly been a flirtation with majority rule devolution and Paisleyism. Finally there had been a return to a rhetoric (the Thatcher/Haughey communiqué) which seemed to envisage a settlement as arising out of some adjustment of relations between the two sovereign governments. It is hardly surprising that there was much Unionist talk of 'Foreign Office conspiracy.' These fears were always exaggerated. As Patrick Keatinge has pointed out, the Unionist 'conspiracy theory' promoted by Enoch Powell depends on the belief that 'sundry intelligence services assiduously misinform their political superiors, all in the interests of a western alliance revitalised by the inclusion of Ireland.'[30] Nevertheless, these fears — faintly absurd though they may have been — had an important side effect. The British government was predisposed to demonstrate its toughness to the Unionist masses by showing a hard face to the demands of the hunger strike movement of 1980, and more especially, 1981.

The Provisionals and Politics: New Developments

Much more significant in the long term than the Atkins initiative was the evidence of a degree of tactical reconsideration within the Provisional Sinn Fein leadership. The IRA's difficulty was not essentially a military one: in 1977 and 1978 it had suffered a large number of setbacks but in the later half of 1978 the Provisionals had reorganised. It divided itself into much smaller units, which paid much greater attention to security.[31] The British Army's mislaid intelligence document 'Northern Ireland: Future Terrorist Trends' (dated 2 November 1978) commented: 'We see no prospect in the next five years of any political change which would remove PIRA's *raison d'être.*' Admiringly, the report observed that 'there is a stratum of intelligent, astute and experienced terrorists who provide the backbone of the organisation.' The document added: 'our evidence of the calibre of rank-and-file terrorists does not support the view that they are merely mindless hooligans drawn from the unemployed and unemployable.'[32] The report did note political weakness — 'there is seldom much support even for traditional protest marches' — but dismissed its significance. 'By reorganising on cellular lines, PIRA has become much less dependent on public support than in the past and is less vulnerable to penetration by informers.'

In fact, the Provisionals were profoundly disturbed by their apparent political weakness. The comments of nationalist journalists reflect this problem. In May 1979 Anthony Cronin noted: 'the fact is that response to the Provisional's appeals on any issue whatsoever, H-Block included, is really dead in the south. Even if the old civil strife and massacre of the Catholics situation were to come about at last, the south would not respond.'[33] In similar vein, Gerry Foley, an American Trotskyist sympathiser, observed of this period: 'the limitations of the Provisionals' campaign had become evident. It was now seen by larger and larger sections of the ghetto population as getting nowhere, more and more out of control, and a source of unnecessary hardship. The Provisionals themselves admitted the appearance of signs of war weariness.'[34] Largely under the impact of Bernadette MacAliskey, the Provisionals in 1978 and 1979 had broken, to an extent, with their political exclusivism. They had been prepared to campaign with others on the issue of 'repression' and the treatment of prisoners. But in the autumn of 1979 these campaigns seemed to have lost momentum. In October Ed Moloney observed in *Hibernia*: 'After last Sunday's Relatives Action Committee sponsored conference in Belfast, to launch a national Smash H-Blocks Committee, Sinn Fein now knows that it is going to be more difficult than they thought to reactivate the flagging H-Block protest campaign.' Noting the Provisional leadership's concern at 'the decline in public interest', Moloney argued that there was one last card available: 'the never quite articulated threat of a hunger strike was in the smoky air last Sunday in speeches from Sinn Fein leaders Gerry Adams and Gerry Brannigan as well as in a letter from the prisoners themselves.' At this point Adams gave an exclusive interview designed primarily to dispel allegations of a 'Marxist plot to swing Sinn Fein to the left.' Adams could hardly have been more frank:

> Q. Is there any Marxist influence on Sinn Fein at the moment?
>
> A. First of all there's one thing which should be said categorically — there is no Marxist influence within Sinn Fein. I know of no one in Sinn Fein who is a Marxist or who would be influenced by Marxism.[35]

As if to prove the point, Adams, when answering questions about the Pope's recent Irish visit and his appeal for peace, did not assert its irrelevance; instead he chose to present the Pope's words as double edged: 'Basically the single issue identified by the establishment was the appeal for peace. . . . the Pope's message was aimed as much at them (the establishment) as at those involved in the resistance movement.' Adams chose to identify himself with the vague, populist (and in practice largely unfulfilled rhetoric) of Irish nationalism.

> Q. Do you not agree though that Sinn Fein has turned to the Left in recent years?
>
> A. I believe personally that to be a Republican in the true sense that you have to base it on the 1916 declaration which in itself is a radical document. It talks about the wealth of Ireland belonging to the people of Ireland. Also as radical was the democratic

programme of the First Dail. If we are to be true Republicans
we have to adhere to what it says in those documents. Our
form of Republicanism is radical Republicanism. We
genuinely believe that when the struggle for independence is
completed and the democratic process re-established, the best
solution is decentralised socialism and government structures.

The document citied, of course, had been merely the radical froth
on a revolution which had a profoundly conservative inner
logic.[36] This type of 'social republicanism' has had a long career
in Ireland; it has influenced the IRA at various times; it has
spawned 'surge' parties of protest (Clan na Poblachta in 1948 was
the most notable example); it is very important to the Irish
Labour Party which has, however, a record of timidity second to
none. It has even influenced key figures in Fianna Fail, the
natural governing party in Ireland. As far as social issues were
concerned, Adams could hardly have chosen to present himself
in a less frightening light. Adam's resolute rejection of Marxism
was clearly designed to open up the space for a degree of populist
social activism on the part of Sinn Fein. Here he was haunted
above all by the charge that he was following the same route as
the despised 'Officials.' After the Republican split, he noted of
the Provisionals:

> There was a natural reaction to stay away from social issues and to
> keep zeroing in on the national question. As confidence has
> grown, people have realised that you also have to push on social
> and economic issues — that you can't simply project the position
> of British imperialism without trying to show people how it affects
> their everyday lives.[37]

Despite Adams' best efforts to explain Sinn Fein policy he was
still widely misunderstood or perhaps misrepresented. W F
Deedes, one of Mrs Thatcher's more prominent supporters in the
media, managed to get it wrong even at the level of simple
reportage: 'The PIRAs are determined, confident, ruthless and far
more ambitious. Their aim is no longer 'Brits Out' but as Adams
has recently proclaimed quite openly, a Marxist revolution in all
Ireland.'[38] But an even more striking analysis of the Provos came
from Bernard Crick in the following month: 'They are not merely
unpolitical, they are anti-political. They are a militant sect, not

the extremists of a Catholic movement.'[39] Even when Crick wrote these words there were profound reasons for refusing to accept them; but the events of the next four years were to reveal beyond any doubt that they had been, in a fundamental sense, misleading. For the hunger strike movement soon demonstrated both that the Provisionals were profoundly political and that they did indeed function as the extremists of a 'catholic' movement. The plight of the IRA hunger strikers starving themselves to death in order that they might be recognised as political prisoners deeply affected many Catholics and led to an upsurge of nationalist feeling with traditional religious overtones. The main Catholic daily paper, the *Irish News*, was full of obituary notices on the lines of 'God's curse on you, England, you cruel-hearted monster' and invocations of 'Mary, Queen of Ireland.' The remarkable wall murals that began to cover gable ends in many Catholic areas of Belfast displayed religious feeling in many ways, the hunger striker as Christ with rosary beads being frequently portrayed. A typical report of the hunger strike campaign ran as follows:

> 'Now when you all kneel down to say your Rosary tonight, as I know you will do, you'll be praying for Bobby Sands, so we'll say a decade now.' And the young man who a minute earlier led the H-Block chant reverently dealt out a decade of the Rosary.
> A moment before they had been shouting: 'One, two, three, four, open up the H-Block door.' Now on the steps of the Enniskillen Town Hall, the Rosary was said, rhythmic, flowing, automatic and passing Catholic housewives joined in. Prayer and protest are easy companions in Fermanagh.[40]

As early as November 1980 the H-Block committees were turning out parades of mourners 'the likes of which have not been since the great civil rights marches of the 1960s and early 1970s.'[41] The hunger strikers and their supporters, as Richard Kearney was to put it, 'articulated a tribal voice of martyrdom, deeply embedded in the Gaelic, Catholic nationalist tradition.'[42]

The first wave of hunger strikes petered out before Christmas 1980, but the second, and more solidly determined wave, led by Bobby Sands, the Provisionals' commanding officer in the Maze, began in March 1981. A major stroke of good fortune for Sinn

Fein came when Frank Maguire, MP for Fermanagh South Tyrone, died on 5 March, shortly after Sands went on hunger strike, though at first Sinn Fein was slow to see the opportunity thus created. Maguire, a strong traditional Republican and semi-abstentionist, had been regarded as the 'prisoners' candidate' and Sinn Fein were, at first, quite happy to see the election in his place of his brother, Noel, whose politics were exactly the same. Bernadette MacAliskey, however, undermined this arrangement by declaring her own interest in the seat. When the Catholic Bishop of Clogher intervened on Maguire's behalf, MacAliskey made it quite clear that she would only stand down in favour of a prisoners' candidate. Jim Gibney, a Belfast Sinn Fein member took up this notion and convinced the cautious Sinn Fein leadership, who had feared rejection at the polls. Noel Maguire yielded to their 'moral' pressure and on 26 March the successful campaign to have Bobby Sands elected as MP for Fermanagh and South Tyrone began; in truth there was a relatively small political difference between voting for Maguire or Sands but the propaganda effect of the election of a prisoner, a hunger striker and a convicted IRA man was immense.[43]

In June 1981 Sands's colleagues Kieran Doherty and Paddy Agnew were elected to the Dail and, following Sands's death, his election agent Owen Carron was elected as MP for Fermanagh and South Tyrone, despite an attempt at non-sectarian opposition from both the Alliance and Workers' Party, though not from the SDLP. The Provos had by October 1981, to accept Thatcher's determination to refuse to allow 'political status', though they won substantial concessions on clothing and association. More important, the Provos had transformed their own relationship to the Catholic masses. The Thatcher government's strategy had been determined by its previous irresolution and vagueness. From May 1979 through to December 1980 it had apparently adopted three different 'solutions' to the Ulster problem: integration in accordance with the Tory manifesto of May 1979; majority rule devolution in accordance with the Atkins initiative in 1979/80 and, at the end of 1980, improved relationships between the two sovereign governments. This inconsistency had reduced the government's room for flexibility in the face of the hunger strikers' demands. Loyalist paramilitaries remained relatively subdued, as Andy Tyrie put it: 'It's nice to be tough but it would be better to be tough about issues other than this. There are special courts and special legislation, so why can't there be special prisoners?'[44] But the forces of political Unionism — both within the OUP and the DUP — had, in different ways, been dismayed by Thatcher's strategy. Her resolution in the face of the hunger striker's demands — no doubt a personal inclination anyway — served to reassure Protestants and to win back ground that her administration had quite casually lost. The *Daily Telegraph*, which strongly supported Thatcher's stand on the hunger strike, acknowledged as much:

> It would be absurd to suggest that the government is wholly to blame for the deteriorating situation in Northern Ireland; but specific misjudgements have been made. It was a mistake to build up Mr Paisley in the pursuit of the chimera of devolved government on the assumption that given the chance he would be a force for moderation . . . . It was a mistake to embark on a bold and imaginative plan on the whole range of British-Irish relations without giving precise indication of the scope of the discussions and without simultaneously calming Unionist fears.
>
> All this constitutes, let it be acknowledged, a record of substantial failure on the part of Mrs Thatcher . . . . The time has come for a new note of strength, clarity and purpose in British policy. What is more the need is urgent and can not be allowed to wait on the convenience of British politics.[45]

Bernadette Devlin MacAliskey was left with a residue of distaste. In an interview with Irish American nationalist, Father Michael Doyle, she declared, 'Ten men are dead . . . their blood is on our hands. All our hands. We didn't do enough to save them. I was prepared to go into Long Kesh after Bobby Sands won the election and try to persuade him to end the hunger strike. But the Provos didn't want me to do it. They wouldn't do it. Of course the prisoners were very strong. It is said the hunger strike built up the movement. There has been a lot of support and money. But ten died — it's a terrible price.'[46] In the same interview she commented icily: 'It is remarkable how many of these boys want a little power. Even the sinners (*sic*) (members of Sinn Fein) are getting into it.'[47]

Sinn Fein had certainly received a major boost to its electoral fortunes. Some allies had performed reasonably well in the 1981 council elections,[48] but it was the 'rolling devolution' scheme launched by James Prior,[49] Atkin's unwilling successor, which provided the opportunity for an apparently dramatic Sinn Fein electoral breakthrough. The 'rolling devolution' scheme was conceivably the last possible variant of a devolutionist strategy. Prior's White Paper of 5 April 1982 had proposed the election of a 78 member assembly whose task was to reach agreement on how devolved powers should be exercised, but for this to occur a 70% agreement was required.[50] The SDLP, though they fought the assembly election in October 1982, decided to boycott Prior's assembly. The results did yet more damage to hopes for any internal accommodation. The official Unionists, so despised during the Atkin's initiative, polled well (29.7) against the DUP (23.0), thus demonstrating in part the soothing effect of Thatcher's stand on the hunger strike and the Falklands on Protestant susceptibilities.

The two parties most committed to dialogue, the Alliance Party (9.3) and the Workers' Party (2.7) won (12%). But in international terms, the most striking result was Sinn Fein's (10.1%) performance, as against that of the SDLP (18.8%) The SDLP had, in fact, slightly increased its vote as against the May 1981 district council elections, but inevitably the sight of a political party attempting, with some apparent success, to combine a ballot box with a military strategy dominated comment.[51] From this point onwards, many observers were obsessed by the fear that the Provisional leadership under 'young Turk' or even it was said, 'young executive' leadership would displace the SDLP as the main voice of northern nationalism.

In the June 1983 Westminster elections, the OUP (34.0) widened its lead over the DUP (20.0) but most emphasis was again placed on Sinn Fein's performance, 102,000 votes and 13.4% of the poll as against the SDLP's 137,012 and 17.9%.[52] In fact, the greatest decline in electoral support for the SDLP had taken place in the 1975-9 period, when there had been a drop of 23.7% to 18.2%; measured against this decline, that of the period 1979-83 when the Sinn Fein challenge emerged, was only 1.6%. But most commentators preferred to focus their attention on Gerry Adams, the avatar of the alleged modernization and radicaliz-

NI Election Results 1973–83 (exc.' 75 Gen. Election)

	1973 (Assembly)	1975 (Convention)	1977 (Local)	1979 (General)	1981 (Local)	1982 (Ass)	1983 (Gen)
Off. Unionist	12.4* 26.5+	25.8	29.6	36.6	26.5	29.7	34
UPNI (Faulknerites)	–	7.7	2.5 N/A	1.9	–	–	–
DUP	10.8	14.7	12.6	10.2	26.6	23.0	20
Vanguard	10.5	12.7	1.4	–	–	–	–
UUUP	–	–	3.2	5.7	N/A	1.8	–
Other Loy'.	1.6	1.5	2.3	N/A	3.3	3.9	N/A
Alliance	9.2	9.8	14.4	11.9	8.9	9.3	8
NILP	2.6	1.4	0.9	–	1.5	–	–
RC/WP	1.8	2.2	2.5	1.7	1.8	2.7	1.9
SDLP	22.1	23.7	20.6	18.2	17.5	18.8	17.9
Combined H Block	–	–	–	–	7.7	–	–
Sinn Fein	–	–	–	–	–	10.1	13.4

N/A = Non Avaiblable *= Anti White Paper += pro-Faulknerite.

ation of Sinn Fein, who was elected MP for West Belfast.[53] It was now presumed in many quarters that the surge of Sinn Fein was irresistible. 'The fact is that muleheaded exclusion of the SDLP by Northern Unionists has played directly into the Provisionals' hands, leaving John Hume's battered machine nowhere to go.' As one Derry journalist tersely commented recently: 'All Gerry Adams had to do is not get killed and he can't lose.'[54] But it was not to be: despite the greatest of all electoral assets — being the victim of an unsuccessful assassination attempt — Adams and his forces were soon to be checked. Sinn Fein's Danny Morrison (91,476 votes) was heavily outpolled by John Hume (151,399 votes) in the European election of June 1984. Hume fought a subtle campaign which effectively surrendered much nationalist territory to the Provos and which sought, instead, to win — successfully — moderate Catholic support away from other parties and thus swell his total. Morrison had written in *An Phoblacht* of the 5 April of the 'political blossoming of the Republican movement in unmistakable radical terms', but his campaign laid its principal stress on more traditional Irish themes ('One Ireland, one people — the only alternative' was the key slogan) topped up with 'clientelism', and 'Sinn Fein now has 28 advice centres.'

After Morrison's defeat, a series of conflicting rationalisations were offered. At first Adams argued that the defeat, (a fact which he regretted,) was due to Provisional over estimation of Catholic toleration of violence.[55] For, whilst overall violence had declined, under 'young Turk' leadership the Republican share had substantially increased, with British soldiers providing a minimal proportion of casualties, the great majority being either local Protestants (UDR or RUC) or, to an increasing extent political opponents.[56] In an interview with *Magill* magazine in September 1984, Morrison seemed to take a different view. 'The thing I have to emphasise, that all republicans are united on,' he said 'is that electoral politics will not remove the British from Ireland. Only armed struggle will do that . . . I think there's very litle reason for the IRA to lower its range so to speak.' Adams had by this time adopted yet another line — it might be a bad thing he declared, to take over from the SDLP as the catchall party for Catholics as this would inevitably lead to a diminution in social radicalism.[57]

Then again, it was declared by Adams that it might be a bad idea to take over from the SDLP as this would lead to some kind of British constitutional initiative which would probably delude many northern nationalists.[58] Pleasantly whimsical though these speculations may have been — were it not a matter of life and death — they seem to have caused much annoyance within the ranks of the Provo military men, who were naturally somewhat surprised[59] by the sudden presumption that defeating the SDLP was not a good idea after all.

Hume's victory, which had a considerable personal element, still leaves open the very real possibility that his party might fare badly in the 1985 May local council election and after; British suggestions that the recent tightening of the electoral law against impersonation will lead to a 20% fall in the Sinn Fein poll are clearly absurd. The problem for the Adams leadership is not that it may not be able to reactivate its electoral surge: it lies rather in the bankruptcy of its strategic options beyond that point. Notwithstanding the Sinn Fein talks with Clive Soley, Labour's spokesperson, shortly before the Brighton bomb,[60] the Sinn Fein gamble on the Labour left appears increasingly to be unlikely to yield success because of the balance of forces both in the parliamentary Labour party and the electorate at large. Neil Kinnock's recent declaration that Labour's Irish policy of unity by consent could not be achieved for 'many, many decades'[61] was symptomatic here. Despite the illusion that the Provos have a demonic leadership, intelligent, ruthless and far sighted, as compared with flabby democratic politicians — a notion fostered particularly by Conor Cruise O'Brien[62] — there must be some doubt, as a recent observer has pointed out, as to whether there is a 'coherence of strategy and organisation, an all pervading logic and an integrated military plan.'[63] Regardless of all disavowals, the Provos are now trapped to some degree in the search for electoral approval, whilst any renewed electoral success is likely to generate more problems for the Irish than the British government.[64]

The Forum Report

The decision to establish the New Ireland Forum in 1983 was clearly related to a pressing and immediate political crisis, namely, the threat posed by the rise of Sinn Fein to the SDLP, the party of constitutional nationalism in Ulster. The SDLP leadership pressed the Irish government for a helpful initiative and the Forum was the response. The Forum was designed to represent the Irish 'democratic' parties. After intensive investigation, it was intended to deliver a joint statement of the principles believed to be at stake in Ulster. But the Forum had a deeper and more profound cause. Since the collapse of the Irish parliamentary party in 1917, mainstream Irish nationalism had been remarkably devoid of creative proposals on the north. Whatever its other defects (from a republican point of view) the demand for home rule, as promoted by the Irish parliamentary party in its era of dominance (1880-1918), did have one principal merit. Because all home rule schemes assumed some remaining constitutional link between Dublin and London it was thus easier to envisage within this framework (as opposed to that of an Irish Republic) forms of arrangement which reduced, at least, the' fears of both Protestant and Catholic communities in the north. Thus, for example, William O'Brien, a prominent though unorthodox nationalist MP, argued that Ulster's Unionist MPs at Westminster ought to retain a suspensory veto over the legislation of a Dublin parliament.[65] O'Brien regarded this as an extreme concession but one which was necessary to avert the greater evil of partition. Eamon Phoenix has recently shown that, in 1916, when partition became inevitable, Joseph Devlin, the popular leader of the North's embattled nationalists, argued from a different angle: the partitioned area should be confined to the four counties where Unionists had a clear majority and that Westminster, not a local parliament, under the scrutiny of the eighty or so remaining nationalist MPs, should govern this area.[66] After 1921, however, such proposals were inevitably forgotten.

It has recently been argued that de Valera's views on Ulster were more flexible 'revisionist' even, than many of his nationalist admirers may have presumed.[67] But there was nothing in his record on Ulster which compared with the contributions of either O'Brien or Devlin. Symptomatically, John Hume had to return to the 'discredited' legacy of the old parliamentary party when, at the SDLP conference in Belfast in 1984, he was casting around for a suitably conciliatory advocacy of dialogue between Unionists and Nationalists.[68] He quoted approvingly a speech given by Parnell in Belfast in May 1891, a speech which had incidentally aroused much ire amongst the majority of nationalists.

> I have to say this, that it is the duty of the majority to leave no stone unturned, no means unused, to conciliate the reasonable or unreasonable prejudices of the minority (cheers) . . . it has undoubtedly been true that every Irish patriot has always recognised . . . from the time of Wolfe Tone until now that until the religious prejudices of the minority whether reasonable or unreasonable, are conciliated . . . Ireland can never enjoy perfect freedom, Ireland can never be united; and until Ireland is practically united, so long as there is the important minority who consider, rightly or wrongly — I believe and feel sure wrongly — that the concession of legitimate freedom to Ireland means harm and damage to them, either to their spiritual or temporal interests, the work of building up an independent Ireland will have upon it a fatal clog and a fatal drag.[69]

The question then remains; judged by this standard how does the New Ireland Forum Report stand up? It was finally published on 2 May 1984 after much labour of research and interview by the Dublin establishment. In section 5.2 the Report declares: 'Attempts from any quarter to impose a particular solution through violence must be rejected along with the proponents of such methods. It must be recognised that the New Ireland which the Forum seeks can come about only through agreement and must have a democratic basis.' In section 5.5 this agreement is said to be necessary because 'it would enable both traditions to re-discover and foster the best and most positive elements in their heritages.' Herein lies the basic internal contradiction of the Report: such a declaration must ring hollow when the presentation of arguments in the Forum document is based on a suppression of the 'best and most positive elements' of the nationalist tradition. The Forum Report is an unimpressive document precisely because it falls below the standards of the most serious nationalist reflection on the problems posed by Ulster Unionism.[70]

In agreeing to partition, the British government is accused of refusing 'to accept the democratically expressed wishes of the Irish people' (3.3), thus establishing an 'artificial political majority in the north.' (4.1). There are two profound weaknesses in this argument: the first weakness is the presumption that a geographic entity is necessarily a political entity. As Father O'Flanagan, Sinn Fein's vice-president in its 1917 heyday expressed it so cogently:

> If we reject Home Rule rather than agree to the exclusion of the Unionist parts of Ulster what case have we to put before the world? We can point out that Ireland is an island with a definite geographical boundary . . . Appealing as we are to continental nations that argument will have no force whatever. National and geographical boundaries scarcely ever coincide. Geography would make one nation of Spain and Portugal; history has made two of them. . . Geography has worked hard to make one nation of Ireland, history has worked against it. The island of Ireland and the national unit of Ireland simply do not coincide.[71]

Later in the year Father O'Flanagan expressed the same idea: 'I agree that the "homogeneous Ulster" of the Unionist publicists is a sham and a delusion. But if there be no homogeneous Ulster, how can there be a homogeneous Ireland? . . . A more accurate description of Ireland for the past two hundred years would be an economic and social duality.'[72] The second major flaw is the refusal to discuss the negative features of the movement for Irish self-determination: the 'seamier side of Irish nationalism',[73] as FSL Lyons put it. Irish nationalism appears only as 'the democratically expressed wishes of the Irish people.' This ignores entirely the powerful and sustained critique by a significant minority of nationalists of the sectarian and undemocratic aspects of nationalist politics in the epoch from William O'Brien to Garret Fitzgerald in this century. O'Brien's tone was particularly striking: 'The only reason that we have ever expressed a tenderness towards our Northern fellow countrymen is that we know that their fears are sincere, and do not spring from a desire for ascendancy, and we will never be a party to the ruthless over-riding of a democracy, who have a right to be consulted and

a right to be heard on matters affecting the common weal.'[74] Even
the most conciliatory passages of the Forum Report are not so
forthright. This suggests the fundamental paradox of the 1984
document's claim that 'the positive vision of Irish nationalism . . . has been to create a society that transcends religious
differences' (4.6) — it disregards the dispiriting experience of
those nationalists who were the most vigorous supporters of this
'positive vision.' Instead it prefers a vision of Irish nationalism
as purely passive, wronged and ill-used — not just in the epoch
of the home rule crisis, but also in the civil rights era (3.14) and at
the time of the power sharing executive (4.1). This document
would have us believe that the calculations of nationalist leaders,
let alone their occasional outbursts of triumphalism, at no point
influenced the responses of Unionists. Such defects raised considerable doubts as to whether the report should be regarded, as
Peter Barry, Irish Foreign minister, put it, 'as a new nationalist
political agenda, which to a remarkable degree is realistic,
generous and flexible.'[75]

To dispute the Forum Report 'history' may appear at first sight
to be a redundant task. Garret Fitzgerald has, in effect, argued
that the historical sections are irrelevant and the substantial
section of the Report is set out in Chapter 8, 'Joint Authority.'
Here the report declares:

> Under joint authority, the London and Dublin governments
> would have equal responsibility for all aspects of the government
> of Northern Ireland. This arrangement would accord equal
> validity to the two traditions in Northern Ireland and would reflect
> the current reality that the people of the North are divided in their
> allegiances. The two governments, building on existing links and
> in consultation with nationalist and unionist opinion, would
> establish joint authority designed to ensure a stable and secure
> system of government.
> Joint authority would give political, symbolic and administra-
> tive expression of their identity to Northern nationalists without
> infringing the parallel wish of Unionists to maintain and to have
> full operational expression of their identity. It would be an unpre-
> cedented approach to the unique realities that have evolved
> between Ireland and Britain.

The popularity of the joint authority notion owed much to the politician Jim Prior brought with him as a junior minister in 1981, the exotic figure — by prosaic local standards — of Lord Gowrie. Gowrie specialised in garrulous, mildly pompous interviews — 'I am in politics to make a contribution to the grammar of daily living' — with mesmerised Irish journalists expounding his 'uniquely philosophical view of politics.' But it is clear that the Dublin government believed that these discourses contained a hint.

Gowrie had, it was said, despite his wholehearted commitment to Thatcherism, retained the friendship and respect of 'a rather surprising spectrum of the intellectual left in Britain.'[76] After such a feat, it seemed, therefore, a relatively simple matter for him to square another circle and solve the Irish question. After much 'thoughtful gazing out of the window of his massive ground floor office in Stormont Castle,' Gowrie gave his conclusion to Barry White of the *Belfast Telegraph*, then to Nicholas Leonard of the *Sunday Press*[77] and then to Mary Holland of the *Sunday Tribune*. With White, 'waving a hand dismissively at a desk scattered with papers', he was at his most 'provocative': 'Direct rule . . . is very unBritish. It is an absurdity that one has almost absolute power . . . I suppose that if I had my way I would have dual citizenship. Why not have people living in the North who regard themselves Irish administered by Ireland and Britain?'[78]

Gowrie was never to expand on his idea, partly because of the horror it induced in the Northern Ireland Office. It was left to Garret Fitzgerald and his allies to develop the notion. Unfortunately, the deficiencies of the Forum Report's historical analysis dogged even its principal proposal for the future. For a major problem with the Report lay in its erroneous and impoverished characterisation of British policy. 'The immobility and short-term focus of British policy — the fact that it has been confined to crisis management — is making an already dangerous situation worse.' Such a simplistic conception — the 'crisis management' phrase has become the defining shibboleth of the Forum's supporters — distorts the real development of British policy since 1972. The administrative integration of Northern Ireland within the United Kingdom bureaucracy is simply ignored.[79] So, almost unbelievably, are the previous negative effects of the

British effort in 1974 to introduce an 'Irish dimension.' The supporters of the New Ireland Forum Report awarded themselves high marks for originality when, in fact, they were repeating exactly the same error — an insistence on an institutional Irish dimension which can not satisfy the demand for Irish unity while at the same time unnerving Protestants — which did so much to sabotage power-sharing in 1974.

The Forum Report might conceivably have been of some significance, in its effect on the long term evolution of attitudes in particular. Instead, by the standards borrowed by John Hume from Parnell, it falls sadly short of its objective, even at the ideological level. Even by the standards of Fitzgerald's abortive 'constitutional crusade' of 1981,[80] it is a disappointment. While Fitzgerald had openly acknowledged the sectarian features of the Republic's life, the Forum Report merely notes that the Ulster Protestants *perceive* these to exist. The immediate prospects for its main political proposal — joint authority — do not appear to be good.

James Prior, the secretary of state from 1981-4, had been somewhat demoralised by the SDLP's boycott of his Assembly — thus reducing it to the status of a mere talking shop for the OUP, DUP and Alliance — and in the darker and more depressed moments of his internal exile was given to speculating about the possibilty of an 'Irish Cuba' and other ill effects of nationalist 'alienation.'[81] Throughout his period in office Prior was said to be sceptical about the pro-Unionist advice he had received from the Northern Ireland Office.[82] He had refused to criticise Gowrie's original support in 1982 of the joint authority idea, and his response to the Forum Report, given in a direct interview with the Belfast *Irish News* is therefore of some interest. It implies a considerable evolution in Prior's personal views: his early toleration of speculative proposals seems to have largely evaporated. Describing his parliamentary response to the Forum Report, Prior declared:

> The British government's response was measured and realistic. We did set out our realities and I personally think that our realities were more real than some of the suggested solutions put forward in the Forum Report. They seemed to beg a question the whole time saying that nothing can be done without consent. That is the

weakness of the Report . . . I don't think parliament or West-minster or Great Britain is particularly concerned about the Forum Report. Generally speaking, realities are put in, in wide enough terms it is rather like motherhood, everyone is in favour of motherhood: and I think in a way can be in favour of the realities.[83]

In the same interview, Prior was sceptical of the alleged security benefits of the joint authority proposal: 'I am convinced it would not be easy to get elements of the Catholic community to respect any force of law and order.' Prior gained an unlikely but effective ally in the leader of the revived Irish opposition, Charles Haughey. Haughey observed of joint authority: 'All you would have would be the Irish government helping the British govern-ment to rule the six county area, over which the British would retain sovereignty . . . the advocates of Joint Authority are looking for it in the security area. That in my mind, would be a recipe for civil war in the north, with spill-over effects in the south.'[84]

The joint authority proposal finally received the *coup de grâce* from Douglas Hurd, Prior's successor, in his speech to the Con-servative Party Conference on the day after the Provisionals' bomb blast at Mrs Thatcher's hotel. Hurd declared that all *three* of the Forum's models were unacceptable, including the joint authority proposal. Fitzgerald's own negative response to the proposal by two academics, Kevin Boyle and Tom Hadden, for a cross border security system,[85] seemed to mark his own final slightly disingenuous retreat from ideas with which he had himself been associated.[86] Even more worrying for Irish nationalism was the revelation in the *Sunday Press* of Dublin on 4 November that Mrs Thatcher had — in a period when she was supposed to have been considering the Forum Report — twice asked her civil servants to draw up documents on repartition. The administrators, understandably horrified by the prospect, had refused. Nevertheless, this was a sobering development: while there remains a democratic majority for partition no British government is likely to deny its validity. However, many of the Forum participants clearly believed that demographic changes which will create a nationalist majority in Northern Ireland are under way;[87] in such an event, some Unionists, though not Paisley, have threatened repartition (to create a secure if smaller Protestant enclave); such an objective would, however, split both Ulster Protestants and the British state. Nevertheless, Mrs Thatcher's action and the words of some Unionists leaders show that it is not an impossible outcome.

Nationalists who seek a United Ireland might well ponder the fact that the most likely route is by deepening a self-critical politics of conciliation — the Forum represents only the most hesitant beginning here — in order that British and Ulster-based opposition to re-unification, in the event of a democratic majority for it, might be reduced as far as possible. They could do worse than re-discover William O'Brien's legacy and revive his project — which was designed to do precisely this. It should not be forgotten by those who see O'Brien and his All for Ireland League of MPs solely as misguided idealists, that his policies were designed — by showing ample evidence of nationalist good faith towards the Protestant community — to create the conditions in which British intervention against the most sectarian Unionists might be achieved.[88]

The Thatcher-Fitzgerald summit of November 1984 appeared to mark the end of an era: an era when discussion had been dominated by highly speculative proposals of the joint authority type.[89] Given Haughey's firm opposition — which probably explains the marks of British favour[90] he received in this period, and Fitzgerald's increasing incoherence — the British had little option, even if they had wanted to embrace the proposal. The unofficial Kilbrandon report which had attempted to give some substance to the joint authority idea was still-born.[91] The NIO position, accepted by both Hurd and Thatcher, was clearly defined: 'far reaching moves could be dangerous in that they might stir a backlash without actually solving the problem of the alienation of the minority in the north.'[92] Even more decisively, the long awaited British response to the Forum Report was postponed *sine die*. 'In London it is said that to go through the Forum Report line by line, saying which parts the British agree with, and which parts they don't would inevitably only highlight disagreement.'[93] Instead closer co-operation was sought primarily on security matters, though the possibility clearly existed of a purely consultative role for the Irish government in the north. Joint authority had always been a profoundly idealist

solution ot the Ulster question — not because there were not
two national identities in conflict but because it offered only a
means of intensifying that conflict by heightening uncertainties
and expectations on both sides.[94] It has been implied that there is
a way forward simply by breaking with obviously dated and
incoherent notions of sovereignty: 'Lives are being lost for want
of a new edition of the textbook'[95] was how the *Guardian* edi-
torialist myopically responded to the Darkley massacre of pen-
tecontalists by 'socialist republicans.' There is no conception
here of a programme to overcome material Catholic disadvan-
tage in Ulster. Symptomatically, the most ardent supporter of
joint authority within the government, Gowrie, is a vigorous
supporter of the main elements of 'Thatcherism's' economic
strategy. The strategy of the Irish political establishment and its
sympathisers deserved little better than the rebuff it received
from Hurd. But this is decidedly not the same thing as saying
that the needs of the Northern Ireland people can be met by
another bout of business as usual. One of the most negative
effects of the recent political agenda of Irish nationalism has been
the suppression of the issue of structural reform: significantly,
one of Prior's aides has recently recalled that when the then
Secretary of State asked Hume for his 'shopping list' the SDLP
leader retreated into a 'Celtic mist.'[96] It is to this problem which
we now turn.

NOTES

1. J Cole, 'Humphrey's Unhappy Heritage', *Observer* 27 June 1979.
2. The *Economist* 7 July 1979.
3. See Adrian Guelke's valuable paper, 'The American Connection to the
Northern Ireland Conflict,' *Irish Studies in International Affairs* vol. 1, No 4, 1984,
p. 34.
4. Henderson's statement came the day after a major speech by the newly
elected leader of the Official Unionist party, James Molyneaux, in which he had
ruled out the possibility of devolved government within the next five years and
had argued that his party should concentrate on improving direct rule. See
Guelke ibid.
5. See Sean Cronin's three articles on Irish America (*Irish Times*, 8-10 October
1984) which lament the passing of the 'Irish vote', note the inability of any Irish
issue since 1968 to mobilise a crowd of more than 10,000 and estimate those Irish
Americans interested in Irish politics at about 100,000, out of an ethnic community of over forty millions.
6. Mrs Thatcher, interviewed in the *New York Times* 12 November 1979.

7. The *Guardian* 20 February 1980.

8. The Government of Northern Ireland: A Working Paper for a Conference (Cmnd 7763).

9. *Belfast Telegraph* 22 November 1979.

10. Mary Holland, 'Thatcher's Initiative Becalmed', *New Statesman* 30 November 1979. The same writer, somewhat inconsistently, has recently declared that the Provo relationship to the SDLP is that of 'worst enemies' *New Statesman* 26 October 1984.

11. ibid.

12. ibid.

13. 'Parnell's authority did not rest only upon the number of votes at his disposal, but mainly on the terror which every Englishman felt at the bare announcement of agrarian troubles. A few acts of violence were exceedingly useful to the Parnellian policy . . . a parliamentary group sells peace of mind to the Conservatives who dare not use the force they command'. G Sorel, *Reflections on Violence*, New York 1972, p. 82

14. See Paul Bew, *Land and the National Question in Ireland 1858-82*, Dublin 1978.

15. *Economist* 7 July 1979.

16. At the press conference following the publication of the Paper, Humphrey Atkins was asked what he would do if the SDLP raised the 'Irish Dimension' at the conference: Atkins replied that 'he would rule it out of order.' (*Irish Times* 21 November 1979). In order to obtain SDLP participation, however, Atkins was forced to concede the principle of parallel talks allowing the SDLP to invoke the Irish dimension.

17. On Paisley's maneouvres at this juncture, see the bizarrely entitled *Paisley on the Lundy Trail* (Belfast 1981) by the pro-integrationist *Workers Weekly* group, which contains all his key speeches and statements.

18. Peter Jenkins, 'The Way Forward', *Guardian* 20 February 1980.

19. ibid

20. *Economist* 23 February 1980.

21. *Economist* 20 October 1979.

22. *Guardian* 20 February 1980.

23. *Economist* 14 June 1980.

24. *Economist* 28 June 1980.

25. *Economist* 20 July 1980. The *Belfast Telegraph* poll (11 October 1984) noted that 58% of the Protestant population claimed to be 'basically satisfied' with direct rule as against 50% of the Catholic population.

26. *Economist* 22 November 1980.

27. Peter Jenkins, *Guardian* 20 February 1980.

28. *Economist* 26 July 1980.

29. ibid.

30. P Keatinge, *A Singular Stance: Irish Neutrality in the 1980s* (Dublin 1984) pp.79-80.

31. J Cole, 'Humphrey's Unhappy Heritage', *Observer* 27 June 1979.

32. C Walker 'Bright future for the terrorists', *Spectator* 14 July 1979.

33. *Magill* May 1979 p. 19.

34. *Callaghan's Irish Quarterly* vol. 1, No. 1 p. 14 'Bernadette and the Politics of H-Block.'

35. *Hibernia* 25 October 1979.

36. See, on this point, David Fitzpatrick's classic study, *Politics and Irish Life*, Dublin 1977.

37. *Hibernia* 25 October 1979.

38. W F Deedes 'The Changing Face of Ulster,' *Daily Telegraph* 13 November 1979.

39. 'The pale green internationalists', *New Statesman* 7 December 1979.

40. *Irish Times* 4 May 1981.

41. *Economist* 29 November 1980.

42. *Myth and Motherland*, Field Day pamphlet, No. 5, Derry 1984, p. 12.

43. Gerry Foley 'The Making of a Martyr', *Magill* May 1981, is the best analysis of these developments, though for an excellent general analysis, see Andy Wilson, *The Hunger Strike in Irish History*, unpublished MSc thesis, Queen's University, Belfast 1985.

44. *Fortnight* July 1981, p. 13.

45. *Daily Telegraph*, 20 April 1981.

46. *The Irish Edition* (Philadelphia) vol. 11, No. 10, October 1982, p. 17 A visit to Bernadette Devlin MacAliskey.

47. ibid.

48. S Elliott and F J Smith, *Northern Ireland: The District Council Elections of 1981*, (Belfast 1981), p. 39.

49. Prior was visibly reluctant to be sent to his 'internal exile' in Ulster. It is hardly surprising: Northern Ireland traditionally plays no role in the evaluation of British political leadership of the first rank — to which Prior aspired. No British commentator, not even amongst the ranks of scholarly historians, ever mentions Lloyd George's or Winston Churchill's direct responsibility for the funding and establishment of the partisan security apparatuses of the Northern Irish state (see Bew, Gibbon and Patterson, *The State in Northern* Ireland ch.2). No one mentions, either, Roy Jenkins's lackadaisical performance at the Home Office, which contributed to the later development of the civil rights crisis (see C E B Brett, *Long Shadows Last Before*), Edinburgh and London 1978, p. 135. The defection of Bill Rodgers from Labour to the SDP was provoked by the offer of the shadow Northern Irish post and so on.

50. See Padraig O'Malley, *The Uncivil Wars: Ireland Today* (Boston and Belfast 1983) ch. 11.

51. Turnout 62.6, See *Irish Information Partnership*. Agenda Data Base: Section 2, category C2, for these results.

52. Turnout 72.0, the same source.

53. Though, it is worth noting, on a minority vote, Adams obtained 16,379 against the SDLP's Joe Hendron (10,934) and the SDLP's ex-leader, Gerry Fitt, 10,326. This represented a considerable comeback for Fitt — whose elevation to the Lords had been widely predicted for some time. In the local government elections of 1981 Fitt had polled a mere 541 votes as against 3,006 in 1977.

54. Alan Murdoch, 'The New Ireland Forum', *Marxism Today* May 1984, p. 3.

55. Paul Hainsworth, 'The European Election in Northern Ireland', *Parliamentary Affairs*, vol 37, No. 4, 1984, p. 459.

56. See *Irish Times* article by Jim Cusack, 2 October 1984 or the *Fortnight* editorial of November 1984. Cusack notes that in the first nine months of 1984, the Provos killed 22 Protestant security force members, 6 British soldiers, 1 Catholic ex-UDR man, 1 magistrate and his daughter, and 1 assistant prisoner governer: also 2 alleged informers and 1 alleged criminal. The security forces had killed 5 people and Loyalists had killed four in the same period.

57. *Brass Tacks* interview, broadcast BBC 2, July 1984.

58. *Irish Press* 20 September 1984.

59. *Sunday Press* 14 October, for the best analysis of this point. For the first clear

evidence of this tension, see *Magill* July 1983 where Adams calls for a refinement of IRA activity while a member of the IRA Army Council calls for an 'escalation.'

60. See Morrison's interview with *Magill* September 1984.

61. *Newsnight* BBC 2, 12 October 1984; see also the article by K Toolis, *Irish Times*, 1 February 1985.

62. *Irish Times* 16 October 1984.

63. 'Provo Dilemma', *New Hibernia*, November 1984, vol. 1, No. 2, p. 4.

64. Here we refer to the difficulties that would face any Irish government, but particularly one led by Fitzgerald, continuing to articulate the demand for Irish unity 'by peaceful means' if the party of constitutional nationalism in the north was eclipsed. The Provisionals do not appear to have the capacity or opportunity to launch a major political challenge to the power structure in the Republic — though there is much scaremongering on this score. See Padraig O'Malley's otherwise valuable *Uncivil Wars* pp. 383-96.

65. *The Responsibility for Partition* (Dublin 1921) p. 14.

66. For an excellent discussion of Devlin's position, see Eamon Phoenix, *The Nationalist Movement in Ireland 1914-28*, Queens University of Belfast, PhD Thesis, 1983, 56-8 pp 153-66.

67. J Bowman, *De Valera and the Ulster Question* (Oxford 1982) pp. 303-5.

68. This was a feature of Hume's approach at this time. He had argued that the Forum was not a 'nationalist revival mission' as against Haughey, who called for the 'revival' and 'retention' of 'our fundamental assumptions.' See on this point. R Kearney, *Myth and Motherland* Field Day Pamphlet, No. 5.

69. For the speech and context see Paul Bew, *C S Parnell* (Dublin 1980) pp. 127-31.

70. We are here offering an internalist critique rather than a Unionist one which would reject its basic premises. On the thorny question of whether sections (4.1) and (4.2) effectively abrogate the principle of consent enunciated elsewhere in the Report, see *Workers Weekly*, vol. 2, No. 487, 26 May 1984.

71. *Freeman's Journal* 19 June 1916.

72. *The Leader* 2 September 1916.

73. F S L Lyons, *John Dillon*, London 1968, p. 324.

74. B Clifford ed, *Reprints from the Cork Free Press*, Belfast and Cork 1984, p. 40. James Connolly, it should be noted, was an admirer of this journal.

75. *Irish Times* 24 September 1984.

76. *Sunday Tribune* 14 April 1982.

77. *Sunday Press* 6 March 1982.

78. *Belfast Telegraph* 13 January 1980.

79. See the recently retired head of the NICS, Sir Ewart Bell's comments on this point, *Belfast Telegraph* 29 January 1985, p. 12.

80. Roy Foster, 'Garret's Crusade', *London Review of Books*, January 1982.

81. Adrian Guelke, 'International Legitimacy, Self-Determination and Northern Ireland', *Review of International Studies*, vol. 11. 1985, p. 43.

82. Mary Holland, 'Echoes of the Bomb', *New Statesman* 9 November 1984.

83. *Irish News* 26 July 1984.

84. *Belfast Telegraph* from the *Irish Press* 26 September 1984.

85. See Boyle and Tom Hadden, 'Towards a System of Cross Border Security for Northern Ireland', *Fortnight* November 1984, an edited version of an addendum on security to a discussion paper by Boyle and Hadden, 'How to read the New Ireland Forum Report', *Political Quarterly*, vol. 55, No. 4, October-December 1984, pp. 402-418

86. *Irish Times* 6 November 1984, 'Fitzgerald rules out hot pursuit zone.'

87. Paul Compton *Fortnight*, March 1983 is one academic who is sceptical of this demographic argument, however, see his 'A Catholic Majority Out of Sight.' For an optimistic nationalist view, see Sean Hone, Population Changes in Northern Ireland, *Troops Out of Ireland*, vol. 8, No. 3, December 1984/January 1985, p. 6.

88. See on this point, suggestively, D D Sheehan, *Ireland Since Parnell*, London 1921, pp. 248-9 and W B Wells, *John Redmond*, London 1919, p. 114.

Our discussion here presumes that there is little prospect of Unionist 'consent' being given to a United Ireland short of the formation of Nationalist and Catholic majority within Northern Ireland. As Professor J J Lee, one of the Republic's most serious academic commentators, had commented on the Forum Report: 'The Report fails to confront the reality of the unsuccessful performance of the Irish state. The Republic is . . . an unsuccessful socio-economic entity, having slid down the European league-table of socio-economic achievement since the Second World War. In terms of per capita income, she now occupies a third division all of her own — behind Britain, equally alone in the second division — and far behind the twelve other members of OECD northern Europe. Indeed there would be no third division in north Europe but for the Irish achievement. The Report does not face the question of why anybody should want to join the third division out of their own free will, especially if they are still in the second division themselves, and have been accustomed to thinking of themselves in the first division.' J J Lee, 'Ireland Forum — Forging a new reality', *Administration*, vol. 32, No. 2 1984, p. 120.

89. Symbolised also by the department of Clive Soley as Labour's most voluble Ulster spokesperson. Soley's last major intervention had been a call for 'harmonisation' of north and south leading to unity. Soley had told the *Irish Times* (17 August 1984) of an interesting scheme he had in mind: 'pensions and other social welfare entitlements for the whole of the island would be paid through Dublin, but those for Northern Ireland would be financed by the British exchequer.' Soley did not specify as to whether these payments were to be made at United Kingdom or Republic levels, nor why this postal re-routing of Treasury funds would deceive anyone or affect political attitudes.

90. From the journalist T E Utley and, more notably, the British ambassador in Dublin, *Phoenix* 7 December 1984.

91. The majority of the Kilbrandon team had called for a five person executive to be composed of three Ulster politicians (possibly MEPs) the Foreign Minister of the Republic and the Secretary of State for Northern Ireland. In contemporary terms, this body would consist of Douglas Hurd, Peter Barry, Ian Paisley, John Taylor and John Hume.(!) It is not clear how Barry's participation was intended to reduce the alienation of the Sinn Fein electorate. For the account of the other Kilbrandon proposals, see Anthony Kenny, 'A Chink of Hope in the Irish Gloom.' *Observer* 11 November 1984.

92. D McKittrick, 'Hopes for New Initiative from Summit Fades', *Irish Times* 12 November 1984.

93. *Irish Times* 12 November 1984.

94. Notably in 'The Sovereignty of Parliament and the Irish Question', Bernard Crick's argument for a 'tolerable muddle' in Des Rea (ed), *Political Co-Operation in Divided Societies*, Dublin 1982.

95. *The Guardian* 22 November 1983.

96. 'The Fall from the Summit', *Magill*, December 1984. For a less critical portrayal of Hume, see Barry White, *John Hume: Statesman of the Troubles*, Belfast 1984.

Conclusion

The 'armed struggle' in Northern Ireland is supported by many profoundly conservative people — people whose views are of a traditionalist Catholic and nationalist sort — both in America and Ireland itself. The Provisional IRA would be greatly weakened without this bedrock of sympathy. During the 'pro-life' referendum campaign of 1983, which amended the Irish constitution to bring it more into line with Catholic (though not Protestant) ideology on the question of the right to life of the unborn foetus, strong nationalists tended to be on the side of the triumphant pro-amendment lobby.[1] The Provisional Sinn Fein leadership, which in discussions with the British left likes to stress its 'feminism' and 'non-sectarianism', had reluctantly to watch many of its prominent southern supporters back the 'right to life' campaign.

But there are radicals who would not necessarily accept the values of conservative Irish Catholic nationalism, and who would argue that the 'legitimate struggle' must be prosecuted, in spite of these 'backward' features of traditional Ireland. These radicals base their arguments on three main propositions. The first of these concerns Britain's alleged reasons for remaining in Ireland. Danny Morrison has recently observed: 'The occupation of the North is a net financial loss to, and a considerable drain on, British revenue. And while repressive methods perfected in the six counties on some occasions have been duplicated in Britain, the main concern of Britain here is not as a testing ground but one of maintaining political control.'[2] In the same article, Morrison also notes: 'The British presence, which once made

140

sense in classic imperialist/capitalist terms, can only now be explained in terms of strategic interest, of NATO and can properly be defined as 'political imperialism.'

In similar vein, Tony Benn has argued: 'We should understand that the occupation of Ireland is primarily a defence issue — it is like a curious cul-de-sac frontier of NATO.' According to *Labour and Ireland*: 'He (Benn) is convinced that if the Republic were persuaded to join NATO (something which he remains totally opposed to) then the argument would change within 24 hours, the veto would simply go away.'[3] This analysis explains the prominence given in the literature of the 'Troops Out Movement'[4] to the civil service advice given to the Attlee government in 1949 (embodied in the document PRO C (49)4) to the effect that British defence interests required the maintenance of partition even if a majority in the north supported re-unification. This document, with its casual dismissal of even the most legitimate (albeit abstract) of nationalist aspirations, has deservedly attracted much critical comment. Nevertheless, it cannot be argued on the basis of this one text of 1949 that defence interests remain the decisive clue to Britain's involvement in Ireland. The context in which the document was written has changed markedly. Firstly, the strategic significance of Ireland is now rather less than in the 1940s, when British thinking was dominated by the maritime losses of World War II. Secondly, it has become increasingly clear that Irish governments are prepared to undertake that they will join NATO if the partition question is solved. As early as 18 March 1949, George Garret, American envoy to Dublin, reported a conversation with Sean McBride, Irish Foreign Minister and later a Lenin prize winner, which was revealing on this point: 'Adverting to Atlantic Pact I asked him for clarification if he considered himself committed to Ireland accepting its provisions if partition issue removed. He said there was no, repeat no, question about this and added it would be a logical step to take.'[5] Moreover, as a recent commentator has observed: 'an examination of the advice being submitted by the Department of External Affairs leaves one in no doubt that in 1961, if NATO membership had been a pre-requisite for EEC membership, Prime Minister Lemass and his officials would have swallowed hard and abandoned neutrality.'[6]

William Fitzgerald has recently argued that 'Britain can not afford the loss of the Northern Ireland coastline except in return for all Ireland membership of NATO.'[7] This seemed to be the logic of the then Premier, Charles Haughey's speech in the Dail debate on neutrality in March 1981.[8] Haughey had then advanced the proposition that a re-united Ireland would be in itself of 'significant strategic value to Britain and Europe', and went on to argue that when re-unification occured 'he would, of course, have to review what would be the most appropriate defence arrangements for the island as a whole.' The evidence thus suggests that Irish 'neutrality' is not the decisive obstacle to Irish unity. Indeed, at the time of Sunningdale, the British publicly committed themselves to support for re-unification if a northern majority for it came into being. The Sunningdale formula declared: 'if in the future the majority of the people of Northern Ireland should indicate a wish to become part of a united Ireland, the British government would support that wish.'[9] Thatcher has reiterated this in a recent *Newsweek* interview.[10] The problem remains for the British state: the near impossibility of expelling a million citizens from the United Kingdom — especially in response to a campaign of terrorism.

In the view of many radical republicans, however, Ulster loyalism is passively dependent on Britain. Nell McCafferty, a former civil rights activist and now a prominent Dublin feminist journalist has made this point admirably clear in a recent interview:

> Politically, she supports the Provos and John Hume . . . ' If I were in the north today I would get arms for the Provos but I would hate it all the while. I would like there to be a clean war . . . ' she does not believe that the Loyalists will fight once the British withdraw their support because they know they are wrong . . . the effect of this places her in the odd left position of having sympathy for the Catholic *petite* and *haute* bourgeoisie but not for the Loyalist working class.[11]

This frank statement — which might stand as epitaph for the decline of the ideals of the civil rights movement — is however, based on a mis-apprehension of the role of the British state. Historically, Loyalism has been at its most aggressive and remorseless (1920-5) when British policy was at its most uncertain. It is quite clear from British government papers that, from the onset of a serious armed national liberation struggle in the south of Ireland (1918), the over-riding objective of British ruling-class strategy was not support for Loyalism but the establishment of a moderate independent Dublin government which would exclude De Valera and other consistent republicans. The fate of the Northern Unionists was always considered of secondary importance, to the extent that even those who supported them, such as Winston Churchill, did so because they felt this would ultimately strengthen the Free State party. The British Prime Minister of the time, Lloyd George, sought to undermine the Unionists for precisely the same motive. British acquiescence in Unionist rule did not become a historical fact until the onset of the Irish Civil War (June 1922), in which it was clear from the beginning that the Free Staters held the advantage.[12] Moreover, the British ruling class has remained ready ever since to sacrifice the interests of the Unionists if this seemed expedient — Churchill's 1940 offer to de Valera of national unity in exchange for joining the war is only the most public example.[13] In other words, while the British ruling class has always pursued an imperialist line, this could ally it to different forces at different times. The idea that Loyalism was a reflection, or even a necessary support of imperialism profoundly under-estimates not only Unionism's essentially indigenous basis but also the flexibility of imperialism itself.

The final key element in the radical pro-republican analysis of Loyalism may be found in the idea that Unionism's working-class support is based upon material privileges. The Loyalist proletariat, it is argued, is a labour aristocracy. Leaving aside whether the term 'labour aristocracy' is genuinely applicable in this purely sociological sense, let it be acknowledged that Protestants do enjoy superior 'life chances' relative to Catholics in Northern Ireland — indeed, our recent research has shown how during Unionist rule the position of Catholics systematically deteriorated. It is the political significance of these differences which is in doubt. Consider just one of the difficulties raised by the classic 'socialist republican' view: historically, the most privileged groups of Protestant workers have been the supporters of reformism, not of Orangeism, while the most militantly Orange sections of the population have been the rural proletariat of the border areas and the unskilled and the lumpen proletariat of the town. The political significance of these differences is actually the reverse of that usually suggested. They are the products, not the cause, of a particular kind of Unionist rule.

It is only by disregarding the massive confusions inherent in the radical nationalist perception of the Ulster issue that it is possible to argue that Provisional Sinn Fein under its present leadership has transcended its past defeats. One observer of the party's 1984 conference reported: 'the Provos no longer appeared to be locked into their own past and fighting over arcane points of Republican ideology.'[14] In our view, such an analysis greatly exaggerates the novelty and progressive potential of the Provisional's strategy of combining terrorism with electoralism. Even in 1984, adherence to 'arcane points of republican ideology' proved to be strong enough to jeopardise the leadership's pragmatic desire to recognise the legitimacy of the Republic's political institutions. At a much deeper level, however, the position of the Provisional leadership on all the key questions in the north — the nature of the British state; the impact of terrorism on that state; and above all the supposedly brittle nature of Ulster Unionism — remains as primitive and underdeveloped as at any time since 1969.

The strategic implication of our analysis — that the problem of the involvement of the British state in Northern Ireland lies not in its existence but in its specific forms — will be anathema to many on the Irish and British left. However, let them consider the fact that even the most intransigent opponents of the British state, the Provisionals, favour a substantial increase in British involvement — to effect the disarming of the RUC and UDR — as an essential transitional arrangement. This is only the latest indication of the movement's strategic bankruptcy. For while it is clear that an eventual British withdrawal is not inconceivable, the idea that the British state would become embroiled in a military confrontation with the Protestants to mitigate the problems for what would inevitably be seen as a hostile successor state is grotesquely naive. The only realistic alternative to a continued British involvement is a withdrawal leading to re-partition. Even if we felt that the only likely prospect for Northern Ireland was to continue to be ruled as at present, we consider that this would remain a clearly preferable alternative to the terrible reactionary involution of politics which would result from the emergence of a smaller and homogeneously Protestant state.

It is particularly necessary in this context to be realistic about the state and nature of the local progressive forces. The last twelve years have confounded the hope of some British policy makers that one effect of direct rule and PR would be to break up sectarian voting patterns and to create the space for the emergence of an electorally significant centre in Ulster politics. The Alliance Party has never got more than 14% of the poll and in the 1983 Assembly elections was reduced to 8%. Its electoral support is clearly limited to the east of the province. It is also limited in socio-economic terms — its media image as a middle-class party is largely justified, although there has been some seepage from the Northern Ireland Labour Party in areas like north and east Belfast. Its 'partnership' policies, which emphasise the classical bourgeois values of equality of opportunity and of treatment by the state — undoubtedly progressive in the Northern Irish context — do not have the capacity to undermine the existing political alliances. It is also the case, as was revealed by its evidence to the committees of Prior's assembly that on specific areas like housing, its policies are actually quite conservative.

The 1970s saw the final disappearance of the Northern Ireland Labour Party, which had been able in the early 1960s to win four of the Belfast seats at Stormont. As late as the general election of 1970, in one of its traditional areas of support — North Belfast — its candidate won 18,894 votes, a substantial 31.9% of the poll. In sharp contrast, in 1979 the NILP's three Belfast candidates were only to win 4,411 votes between them. Its decline was a reflection of the degree to which some of its strongest areas of support had been devastated and polarised by violence and intimidation. The party had also been negatively affected by the massive movements of population which took place in the early parts of the troubles. Thus, to give the example of North Belfast again, its total population declined by 27% between 1971 and 1981. The period also saw the intensification of a long period of decline of those traditional industries whose workforces had included a significant number of NILP supporters. In 1970 manufacturing employed 32% of the Ulster workforce — by 1981 the figure was down to 23%. The Northern Ireland Labour Party, which had relied heavily on its links with the trade unions in these traditional industrial sectors, was bound to be affected by this decline especially as the context of acute violence and instability made the recruitment of new supporters impossible. This analysis of the plight of the NILP reveals the impossibility of any other socialist formation simply 'taking its place.' The Workers Party, which has emerged after a long travail out of the 'Official' Republican tradition, is at the stage where it can not hope, in the medium term, for more than the interested attention of sections of the Protestant working class: at the same time, this grouping has been reduced to a hard core of support within Catholic areas where it does, however, continue to expose the gap between the verbose professions of generosity and non-sectarianism of both constitutional and unconstitutional nationalism and the rather seamy reality. (This party's prospects in the Republic are, of course, rather better.)

As we have pointed out in our analysis of the limits of Paisleyism, the British 'presence' particularly as regards the underwriting of post-war economic and social policies, puts a real material limit on the support for reactionary and sectarian politics in the Protestant population. More positively, some of the most significant progressive shifts in Northern politics have been either part of generalised movements of radicalisation in British politics (1917-1921 and 1941-45),[15] or based on demands that Northern 'backwardness' be dealt with (the powerful mobilisations against unemployment and redundancies in 1958-64).[16] In present conditions, where the policies of the British state have done much to exacerbate sectarianism and where the forces representing the politics of democratic accommodation and anti-sectarianism are weak, the prospect may appear bleak. However, we would argue that in an important sense they are no bleaker than those which face the left in the rest of the United Kingdom. For it is precisely in the fundamental re-thinking of left strategy, particularly in the area of a governmental programme that would break with the debilitating legacy of the Wilson and Callaghan years, that an essential pre-requisite for the development of new political alliances within Northern Ireland lies.

Those sections of the left in Ireland and Britain who have insisted on defining the debate about the British state in terms of its 'legitimacy' — on the one hand, those favourable to the Provisionals and withdrawal, on the other the CLR (Campaign for Labour Representation), with its claim that integration is itself the 'solution' — have deflected attention from the real strategic options available to a left government. Our analysis has attempted to demonstrate that the Tory/Labour bipartisanship of the sixties and seventies was based on a narrow and self-serving refusal to deal with the real material obstacles to any substantial degree of cross-sectarian accommodation — in particular the degree of structural inequality between Protestants and Catholics in the economic sphere. The reforms introduced were undoubtedly significant but their significance lay more in undermining and disarticulating the Stormont regime than in improving the condition of the Catholic masses. We can perhaps grasp just how marginal Northern Ireland actually is to the concerns of the British left from the fact that the justified dismissal of the 'reformist' projects of the Wilson/Callaghan governments does not extend to Northern Ireland, where it is still simplistically argued that 'reform' has been tried and its failure puts the 'national question' on the agenda.[17]

The agenda for a strategy of serious structural reforms is clear. Fundamental to it is a break with the *ad hoc*, palliative approach of the Mason period. As Rowthorn has argued, on the basis of his own systematic analysis of the Northern economy: 'The ideal combination for Northern Ireland would be a vigorous programme for economic recovery in the United Kingdom as a whole, together with a strong regional policy for directing investment towards the province.'[18] This approach has been rejected because it is claimed that it is 'economistic' and/or treats the north as just another depressed region in the United Kingdom.[19] This would only be the case if it was being argued that economic development would of itself provide a 'solution'. Such a strategy would be complementary to a *specific* attack on structural inequality, but would clearly be the essential basis for the latter. The blatant failure of all the post-69 reforms to infringe on some of the most ingrained patterns of inequality continues to provide a reservoir of resentments for articulation by nationalist politics. There is clearly plenty of room for government intervention in the fields of discrimination (even in government employment there remain serious difficulties)[20] and civil liberties (the setting up of a completely independent procedure for investigation of complaints against the RUC).

The McCrudden Report on the Fair Employment Agency has pointed out that it is understaffed and underfinanced in comparison with the Labour Relations Agency in Northern Ireland, or the Commission for Racial Equality in Britain. In other ways too an absence of commitment on the part of the government has been in evidence. One of Thatcher's junior ministers, Hugh Rossi, attempted unsuccessfully to persuade FEA chairman Bob Cooper to drop a planned inquiry into the Northern Irish civil service, in exchange for a commitment by the government to encourage the granting of government contracts to firms signing the FEA's equality of opportunity declaration and showing a willingness to open their personnel records for FEA inspection. In fact, this is a critical period for the NICS. Catholic recruitment *has* risen markedly since 1973, from 15.0% of the total to 30.5%, but Catholics are still concentrated in the lowest grades; the higher grades remain overwhelmingly (over 80%) Protestant. More generally, McCrudden has argued that the FEA has failed to enforce its legal powers and has relied too much on responding to the complaints of individuals.[21]

A similar sluggishness has existed in the investigation of complaints against the RUC. In 1981 the number of complaints against the RUC rose to 1,715, an increase of 19.3%, but the number actually investigated *fell* by 21% (519), which led to 31 cases of disciplinary action.[22] Despite the obvious doubts raised by these figures, the Northern Ireland Office continues to oppose the principle of independent investigation. In this same area, it is worth noting that the Kilbrandon Report grouping, despite its profound division over the joint authority proposal, did accept the case for the repeal of the Flags and Emblems Act and a restructuring of the security forces to allow for a phasing out of the UDR. This latter proposal has clearly been seriously entertained within the senior ranks of the RUC.[23]

However, it is the economy that is the most vital area for action. It may be argued that such a project is utopian, as the British state has not the capacity or determination to deal with Protestant resistance. Our answer to that is twofold. First, intervention in the economy would clearly provoke much less resistance than attempts to reinforce some new constitutional arrangement, as such a reformist initiative would *divide* rather than unify the Protestant population if it was linked to an economic programme of reconstruction. It is worth noting that the then Labour spokesperson on Northern Ireland, Clive Soley, in presenting evidence to the New Ireland Forum, had no compunction in contemplating the use of force to deal with Unionist resistance to some 'joint authority' solution — 'At the end of the day I can say to you if we are prepared to put in enough troops we have got the power to deal with any situation.'[24] If a representative of the present Labour leadership can contemplate the use of force to ensure for the southern bourgeoisie a share in ruling the North, our own proposals remain minimalist by comparison.

There is clearly no certainty about either the victory of the Labour Party in the next general election or, in the event of such a victory, of a government which will break with the debilitating legacy of the Rees/Mason era. The condition of massive economic devastation and the pressing demands of other regions would make those of Northern Ireland, which has no effective representation in the Labour Party, clearly problematic. The crisis of British Labourism could, it may be argued,[25] make even the consideration of such possibilities redundant. However it is crucial to register the very dislocation of progressive strategic concerns in Northern Ireland from those in Britain. This does open up some real if limited possibilities even under a government dominated by the centre and the right of the Labour Party. Such a government would already be subject to more serious internal pressure on the north than any of its predecessors due, in part at least, to the reaction against the Mason period. So far the critique of this episode has usually been based on uncritical Nationalist assumptions and on slipshod investigation of conditions in the North.

We are arguing for the development of a critical unity on the British left around demands which are far from 'impossibilist,' namely, expansion of the public sector; a serious strategy to deal with structural inequality and the phasing out of the UDR. The implementation of these demands would in no way 'solve' the problem. This can only be done through the disarticulation of the two communal class alliances and is a task for internal socialist and democratic forces. It has been the important theoretical and ideological development of these forces since 1969 which made this book possible.[26] Ultimately any policies adopted by a Labour government can be judged progressive or reactionary insofar as they strengthen or weaken these forces.

NOTES

1. See W Wilson, 'The Roman Catholic Church and the Eight Amendment', Msc Thesis, Queen's University, Belfast 1984.

2. *An Phoblacht/Republican News*, 5 April 1984 p. 14, 'The argument for withdrawal.'

3. *Labour and Ireland*, vol. 2, No. 5, p. 14.

4. See Troops Out Movement, *Close to Home: Lessons from Ireland*, nd pp. 38-9.

5. George Garrett to Secretary of State, 18 March 1948, RG84 US Legations Records (Dublin) File 1949 (Atlantic Pact) Box 703, Washington National Records Centre. We owe this reference to Professor Ray Raymond.

6. R J Raymond, 'Irish neutrality: Ideology or pragmatism?', International Affairs, vol. 60, No. 1, 1983/4, p. 40; see also P. Keatinge, *A Singular Stance: Irish Neutrality in the 1980s* (Dublin 1984) pp. 25-6, and also very usefully on all these themes, pp. 64–83.

7. W E Fitzgerald, *Irish unification and NATO* (Dublin 1982) p. VIII.

8. Keatinge, ibid. p. 31 and 79.

9. 'Irish Scrabble', the *Economist*, 23 February 1980.

10. Adrian Guelke, 'International Legitimacy, Self Determination and Northern Ireland', *Review of International Studies* (1985) 11, p. 37.

11. *Sunday Tribune* 6 May 1984.

12. For an extended documented account see P Bew, et.al, pp. 50-60 and 207-8.

13. W S Churchill, *The Second World War Vol II Their Finest Hour* (London 1949), pp. 498-9.

14. Mary Holland, 'Echoes of the Bomb', *New Statesman* 9 November 1984.

15. See H Patterson, *Class Conflict and Sectarianism* (Belfast 1980) chps. 5-6 and Bew, Gibbon and Patterson *The State in Northern Ireland* (Manchester 1979) chap. 4.

16. Ibid, chap. 5.

17. See Don Flynn, *Which Way to Withdrawal?* A Chartist Collective Pamphlet (London nd)

18. Bob Rowthorn, Northern Ireland: an Economy in Crisis *Cambridge Journal of Economics* 1981, 5, p. 27.

19. Flynn, ibid.

20. Two important areas are the NICS and the Northern Ireland Electricity Service.

21. The reference here is to the report on the FEA made by the Oxford specialist, in anti-discrimination law, Dr Christopher McCrudden, see A Pollock 'The Civil Service Investigation: the FEA's last chance?', *Fortnight* October 1982.

22. See B Dickson, 'RUC Complaints: No Change.' *Fortnight* December 1982.

23. *Irish Times* 16 January 1985.

24. *New Ireland Forum Public Session No. 11*, p. 51.

25. See Francis Mulhern, 'Towards 2000' *New Left Review* no 148, p. 29 for a cogent statement of this position: 'the historically formed set of relationships that we know as Labourism is now being shaken apart . . . '

26. Of particular importance here was *The Irish Industrial Revolution* (Dublin 1977). Also see H Patterson, 'The State of Marxism in Ireland' in *Class Politics: Theoretical and Discussion Journal of the Worker's Party* Autumn 1983.

INDEX

Printed in the United States
by Baker & Taylor Publisher Services